Sense*Able* Strategies

Including Diverse Learners Through Multisensory Strategies

Anne M. Beninghof

Sense*Able* Strategies:
Including Diverse Learners Through Multisensory Strategies

Edited by Francelia Sevin
Text layout and design by Kimberly Harris
Cover design by Kimberly Harris
Cover and Inside Illustrations by Jonathan Machen
"Working the Fortune Teller" Illustration by Ernie Hergenroeder

Printed in the U.S.A.

Published and Distributed by

SOPRIS
WEST
EDUCATIONAL SERVICES

A Cambium Learning™ Company

4093 Specialty Place • Longmont, CO 80504 • (303) 651-2829
www.sopriswest.com

53STRAT/3-05

For my mother, who taught me to be Sense*Able*

About the Author

Anne M. Beninghof, internationally recognized consultant and trainer, has more than 20 years of experience working with students with special needs, in a variety of public and private settings. She has been a special education teacher, faculty member of the University of Hartford and the University of Colorado, and has published several books and videos. Recently, Anne decided to follow her heart and return to the classroom, where she works part-time with teachers and students who are struggling with the learning process. In both her presenting and writing, Anne focuses on creative, practical solutions for more effectively including students with diverse learning needs in general education classrooms.

$\mathcal{T}$able of Contents

Section 2: — The SenseAble Strategies 45

Introduction

What's So SenseAble About Learning Styles?

❧

*T*he saying "Great minds think alike" is familiar to most of us. Yet, good teachers know that this saying isn't really accurate. Every day, teachers are faced with students who demonstrate great thinking in a wide variety of ways. Some students approach a learning task in a step-by-step, linear manner, whereas others begin by looking at the situation as a whole. Some students intuitively know an answer, but others choose to support their thinking with detailed data analysis. Some students need a quiet environment in order to think clearly, but others relish a noisy, less structured learning experience.

Despite this wide variety of approaches, many schools and classrooms continue to operate as if great minds do think alike, expecting and insisting that all students learn and demonstrate their learning in the same manner. Consider the classrooms where lecture is still the primary form of instruction, where students all take the same teacher-made test and are expected to be quiet as they work. Why do these classrooms continue to exist, given the ever-increasing body of research pertaining to learning styles and the brain? Why do some teachers continue to practice according to the "great minds think alike" point of view? One

reason is that some teachers believe that being fair means treating all students in the same way. However, as Howard Gardner (1997), renowned psychologist and researcher, states: "Education has been the idea of uniform schooling ... and it's presumed to be fair. Actually, it is the most unfair thing in the world. We have to individuate education, reaching as many children as possible, in as many ways as possible." Educating children fairly does not mean equally, but means instead meeting *all* children's educational needs.

Perhaps the rallying cry in our schools should be "*Not* all great minds think alike." If this philosophy were embraced, educators may feel compelled to intensify the search for practical, creative ways to put this thought into practice. Energy and staff development could be focused on instructional techniques, curriculum materials, and classroom interventions that reach out to all learning styles.

What We Know

A significant body of research and experience tells educators that students do not all think or learn alike. This diversity in learning is often referred to as "learning style." "Learning style" is used in many different ways, by different people, but generally refers to a specific combination of factors which influence an individual's ability to learn efficiently and effectively. And, although home and school environments influence learning style, as much as three-fifths of an individual's learning style is biologically imposed (Restak, 1979).

Environment, structure, socialization, time of day, and perceptual input are just a few of the many factors identified as having significant impact on learning. Educators and researchers have developed many learning theory models to identify and describe this wide range of variables that affect learning (see **Table 1**). While these models differ in many ways, they have one thing in common: They all recognize that many different learning styles are present in any classroom.

At a minimum, teachers can expect these learning variations in their classrooms:

- ❧ Perceptual input

- ❧ Time of day

- ❧ Sociological conditions

Students have a variety of preferences for perceptual input. Perceptual input refers to the way in which people receive and comprehend information through their senses. Surprisingly, fewer than 20% of students prefer auditory input in learning situations. The vast majority percieve new information most effectively through their visual, tactile, and kinesthetic senses. Clearly, the prevalence of lecture in today's classrooms does not match dominant perceptual input learning styles.

As to the best time of day for learning, research suggests that about half of any group of learners function best in the morning, with the other half being more successful in the afternoon or evening (Price, 1980; Callan, 1998). Though patterns shift somewhat as schoolchildren age, many students experience strong energy highs in the afternoon or evening. However, elementary school teachers consistently report that basic academics are emphasized in the morning. Secondary schools have generally completed two-thirds of their school day before noon. Therefore, there is a mismatch for many students between their learning style and the structure of the typical school day.

Learners also show sociological preferences. Some students prefer to learn in groups; others prefer to learn on their own. No matter what the preference, research supports the conclusion that when students are permitted to learn through their own sociological preferences, achievement and behavior improve (Andrews, 1990). Recent cognitive and neurological research (Caine & Caine, 1997) suggests that everyone's brain "is a social brain" (p. 19). Classrooms in which students do not have frequent opportunities to learn interactively with others leave many students with unmet needs.

Table 1: Models of Learning Theories

Name	Developer	Style Variables	Reference
Multiple Intelligences	Howard Gardner	Linguistic Interpersonal Intrapersonal Mathematical Logical Spacial Bodily-Kinesthetic Naturalist	Gardner, 1993 Armstrong, 1994
4MAT	Bernice McCarthy	Experiencing Reflecting Conceptualizing Doing	McCarthy, 1997
Learning Style Inventory	Rita Dunn & Kenneth Dunn	Sound Light Temperature Design Motivation Persistence Responsibility Structure Self Pair Peers Team Adult Varied Perceptual Intake Time Mobility Global/Analytical Hemisphericity Impulsive/Reflective	Dunn, Dunn, & Price, 1989
Integrated Intelligence Menus	Harvey Silver, Richard Strong, & Matthew Perini	Mastery, Interpersonal, Understanding, and Self-Expressive *within* each of the Multiple Intelligence components	Silver, Strong, & Perini, 1997

Although there are many students who do well in traditional schools regardless of their learning styles, many students struggle through their school experience. Research on students who are low-achieving and high school students who dropout (Dunn, 1988; Dunn & Dunn, 1993; Mohrmann, 1990) shows these students often have seven learning style characteristics in common:

1. Need for frequent movement

2. Preference for receiving instruction later in the day

3. Need for materials and instruction with a heavy emphasis on tactile, visual, and kinesthetic input

4. Preference for variety in seating, grouping, and environments

5. Need for an informal classroom design

6. Poor auditory perception and memory

7. Preference during elementary and middle school years for dim lighting

Though research dealing specifically with the learning styles of students with disabilities is slim, findings are similar to research on students who are at risk (Yong & McIntyre, 1992). In addition, most special and general educators are quick to agree that the aforementioned seven learning style factors are also applicable to students who have been officially identified as in need of special education.

In reflecting on the needs of students receiving special education, Thomas Armstrong (1987) writes, "Nowhere in this litany of deficit, disability, and disease is there the recognition that these children may learn very well *in their own way*." In later work (1995) Armstrong actually suggests that Attention Deficit Disorder is a myth, developed to account for the many students whose learning styles do not match the most common teaching style: lecture.

Teachers of students with special needs who have attended to individual learning styles have experienced great success. Hodgin and Wooliscroft (1997) report dramatic changes in their inclusive classroom since employing learning style strategies. They found clear gains in academic achievement for students receiving special education, as well as students in regular education. In addition, students demonstrated improved self-esteem, motivation, and attitude toward learning. Brunner and Majewski (1990) reported that since teachers in their high school "began using a learning styles approach, the number of special education students earning regular high school diplomas has grown dramatically."

Given the learning style characteristics of many students who are at risk or receiving special education, it becomes easier to see that traditional classroom instruction will probably not meet their needs. In 1984, author John Goodlad reported that teacher lecture and verbal explanation constituted about one-fifth of the average classroom day. These findings are still supported by visits to today's classrooms. And, unfortunately, the predominance of lecture increases dramatically as students move up through the grades. The majority of high school instruction typically consists of "teacher talk." Even when hands-on materials are available to students, they are often "used indiscriminately rather than with those youngsters whose perceptual inclinations would complement them" (Dunn & Dunn, 1993). Furthermore, research suggests that students who underachieve do so because they are primarily tactile or kinesthetic learners whose "teachers lecture or require reading *as the basic source of introductory learning.*" (Dunn & Dunn, 1993, p. 151). In other words, the mismatch between some students' learning styles and the traditional instructional approach of many classrooms may actually cause learning and behavioral problems.

Thankfully, research also provides good news. Teachers and schools that provide for varied learning styles in planning and implementing instruction yield student success. School districts that have implemented a learning styles approach have seen significant increases in scores on standardized reading assessments (Hodgin & Wooliscroft, 1997; Snyder, 1994) and math assessments (Bauer, 1991). These schools have also seen significant increases in student motivation (Barber, Carbo, & Thomasson, 1994) and attitudes toward learning (Dunn, Giannitti, Murray, Geisert, Rossi, & Quinn, 1990).

Teacher experience supports these results. Students in the primary years, during which tactile and kinesthetic learning are given greater attention, often do fine. As the "teacher talk" increases with the grade levels, students begin to struggle more and more with the material and the learning environment. But, when teachers infuse more variety into the instructional method, lower-achieving students begin to turn around.

What We Can Do

With all of this information, how can educators find a practical, common-sense way to integrate research into practice? Consider this real-life event:

> At a workshop on learning styles, an enthusiastic secondary teacher approached the speaker during the break. The teacher was very interested in the concept of learning styles, but frustrated about how to apply the concept easily and quickly to his classroom instruction. He said, "I like this idea about learning styles, but I have to teach five-paragraph essay writing tomorrow. Can you tell me how to teach that in a multisensory way?"

This is a typical reaction of an educator to learning styles. The idea that every brain is unique and that students have various learning styles makes sense. Teachers are ready to embrace this perspective. But the thought of taking 21 different learning style factors (or the eight multiple intelligences, or any one of the numerous learning style models) and integrating them into daily lesson plans can seem daunting.

This book addresses this seemingly intimidating task by helping educators take the first step by using "sense*Able*" strategies. What exactly are "sense*Able* strategies?" Sense*Able* strategies are reasonable methods to develop student skills by utilizing their sensory strengths. The strategies in this book are organized and based on one major component of learning style: the four sensory modalities. The visual, auditory, tactile, and kinesthetic modalities greatly affect how learners grasp and retain knowledge. These four factors are simple to remember and consider when planning lessons for diverse learners or when modifying instruction and curriculum materials for specific learners. Educators across the United States have successfully embraced these sense*Able* lesson formats and strategies. By focusing on the four sensory modalities used in learning, teachers can quickly and easily include diverse learners.

The purpose of the *SenseAble Strategies* approach is not to train students in one way of learning, but to open up a wider variety of learning possibilities for all students. Although students learn most quickly in their preferred style, it is critical that students learn to cope with situations that do not match their preference. Therefore, this book will guide you and your students in utilizing learning styles information in a variety of ways.

Section 1 provides the background information you need in order to understand and use the *SenseAble Strategies* approach. Chapter 1 suggests methods for assessing your students' dominant and secondary learning preferences. In Chapter 2 ideas are proposed for teaching students about the general concept of learning styles, as well as their own individual styles. Chapter 3 offers

sense	1. the faculty of perceiving by means of sense organs, 2. to be or become aware of
able	1. having sufficient power, skill or resources to accomplish an objective, 2. marked by skill or efficiency
sensible	1. capable of being perceived by the senses or by reason, 2. reasonable, intelligent
SensAble Strategies	
	1. reasonable methods to develop student skills by utilizing their sensory strengths

–adapted from *Merriam-Webster Collegiate Dictionary*, 1974, Springfield, MA: Merriam-Webster Inc.

strategies for engaging families in the learning styles approach. With the awareness and support of families, students' homework, studying, and attitudes toward learning can quickly improve. Chapter 4 provides ideas for lesson planning and Chapter 5 proposes a format for assessing student learning through each of the four senses.

Section 2 of this book describes sense*Able* strategies to use in your classroom. Following each strategy are ideas for adapting the strategy to different content areas, grade levels, or other conditions. Section 2 can be read from beginning to end or simply flipped through until a strategy grabs you. Many teachers begin by thinking about a specific struggling student and looking for ideas which support his or her individual learning style. However, teachers often find that the more they infuse sense*Able* strategies into their whole-group instruction, the less often they need to pinpoint a specific student. Whichever path you choose to start on, if you keep in mind the notion "*Not* all great minds think alike," you are sure to succeed.

Section 1:

The Sense*Able* Approach

Chapter 1

Identifying Your Students' Learning Styles

❧

$\mathcal{T}$he first step in making a senseAble match between instructional style and learning style is identifying the learning styles of your students. With this information you can adjust your teaching, students can be aware of and capitalize on their own styles, and parent(s) can support learning in the home.

There is a variety of methods for identifying learning styles. Start by reviewing any testing previously done with students. For example, many evaluations that determine special education eligibility contain sections identifying learning styles, learning strengths, or learning weaknesses. Test results or evaluator comments might indicate an auditory processing problem, tactile defensiveness, or other difficulties. Although the standard testing information will most often point out perceptual weaknesses rather than strengths, this information can often be used to deduce perceptual strengths. If this information is available, it can be a great time-saver.

The Observation Method

If previous test information is unavailable or does not yield the desired information, another simple method is teacher observation. Even though research has shown that teacher observations may not always provide accurate information for determining all learning style preferences, the areas of greatest accuracy are found to be in the perceptual modalities (Dunn, Dunn, & Price, 1977). Many teachers find that they can identify students as visual, auditory, tactile, or kinesthetic learners simply from their observations in school settings. **Table 2** highlights many of the typical behaviors displayed by students with the four different perceptual strengths. By observing an individual over the course of several days, making comparisons with other students of the same age, and keeping in mind developmentally appropriate behaviors, many teachers can form an accurate picture of a student's strongest learning modality. To best assess a student, ask yourself the question, "What do I see this student doing most often?"

Use **Reproducibles A** and **B** to record your observations of individual students or to group students for a class profile.

If, in addition to the observation method, a standardized tool is deemed necessary, there are many instruments designed expressly for the purpose of identifying learning styles. These

Table 2 : SenseAble Observations

Visual

- Taking copious notes
- Drawing or doodling
- Wanting to look at the pictures accompanying text
- Needing eye contact to listen well
- Choosing visual tasks, such as reading
- Closely examining objects and pictures
- Commenting on the visual aspects of something

Auditory

- Choosing to listen to audiotapes
- Following verbal directions while not appearing to be listening
- Showing a preference for music or singing
- Showing an interest in oral discussions
- Reading aloud to self
- Sounding out words
- Talking to self

Tactile

- Touching objects on shelves
- Fiddling with items in desk
- Carrying small objects around in hand
- Choosing to work with manipulatives whenever possible
- Wiggling fingers frequently
- Grabbing items
- Playing with pencils and pens

Kinesthetic

- Walking around the room
- Standing while working at desk
- Jumping out of seat
- Using body movements for expression
- Enjoying physical education and other movement opportunities
- Volunteering to demonstrate or run errands
- Acting and playing roles

Student Learning Style Observation

Student Name: _____ Date:_____

Teacher: _____

Check the behaviors that you observe the student exhibiting frequently.

Visual

- ❏ Taking copious notes
- ❏ Drawing or doodling
- ❏ Wanting to look at the pictures accompanying text
- ❏ Needing eye contact to listen well
- ❏ Choosing visual tasks, such as reading
- ❏ Closely examining objects and pictures
- ❏ Commenting on the visual aspects of something

Auditory

- ❏ Choosing to listen to audiotapes
- ❏ Following verbal directions while not appearing to be listening
- ❏ Showing a preference for music or singing
- ❏ Showing an interest in oral discussions
- ❏ Reading aloud to self
- ❏ Sounding out words
- ❏ Talking to self

Tactile

- ❏ Touching objects on shelves
- ❏ Fiddling with items in desk
- ❏ Carrying small objects around in hand
- ❏ Choosing to work with manipulatives whenever possible
- ❏ Wiggling fingers frequently
- ❏ Grabbing items
- ❏ Playing with pencils and pens

Kinesthetic

- ❏ Walking around the room
- ❏ Standing while working at desk
- ❏ Jumping out of seat
- ❏ Using body movements for expression
- ❏ Enjoying physical education and other movement opportunities
- ❏ Volunteering to demonstrate or run errands
- ❏ Acting and playing roles

SenseAble Strategies **Reproducible B**

*G*roup Learning Style Profile

Teacher: _____ Date: _____

Write the names of students in the quadrant which most represents their dominant learning style.

Visual	**Auditory**
Tactile	**Kinesthetic**

instruments commonly rely on the student choosing between two or more options, thereby indicating a preference for a certain style. While many tools are available only for readers, some have primary versions that utilize pictures and are also appropriate for nonreaders. Some instruments, such as the Learning Style Inventory (Dunn, Dunn, and Price, 1989/1994) and Reading Style Inventory (Carbo, 1979/1994) have been validated through extensive research. Others have relied on successful classroom use for validation. The following instruments use a variety of approaches in examining learning styles and produce diverse results. (For information about how to obtain these assessment instruments, refer to the Resources section.)

The Learning Style Inventory

The Learning Style Inventory (LSI) is designed to give a comprehensive profile of an individual student's learning strengths and preferences. It presents a series of questions and pictures and asks the student to make a choice from various options. A sample from the LSI primary version appears in **Figure 1.1**. (LSI: P, K-3). The Learning Style Inventory is appropriate for grades 3-12.

The LSI questionnaire assesses preferences for environment (sound, light, temperature, and design); emotional factors (persistence, responsibility, structure, and motivation); sociological factors (working with an adult, alone, or with peers); and physiological factors (visual, auditory, tactile, or kinesthetic perceptual strengths, intake, time of day, and mobility). After the student completes the inventory, a Learning Style Profile is generated from which appropriate instructional strategies can be determined. (See Resources for ordering information.)

Figure 1.1: Sample from the Learning Style Inventory

The Reading Style Inventory

The Reading Style Inventory (RSI) was developed by Marie Carbo in 1979. It differs from the LSI in that its focus is on the learning style factors most likely to help individuals learn to read and become good readers. The RSI is a multiple choice questionnaire given to individual students or small groups. It assesses learning style elements, including environmental, emotional, sociological, and physical stimuli. The primary version includes pictures of children involved in various activities (see **Figure 1.2**) about which the tester questions the student verbally. (e.g., "Do you like to spend a lot of time cutting and pasting things?"). The student marks the picture that corresponds with his or her answer. Test results can be entered into an RSI computer program that delivers a profile of the student's reading style and recommended instructional methods and materials. Using the program, group profiles can also be compiled which provide the classroom teacher with a summary of the learning styles and needs of the class as they relate to reading. (See Resources section for ordering information.)

Figure 1.2: Samples from the Reading Style Inventory

4MAT

The 4MAT approach to learning styles was developed by Bernice McCarthy (1981) and is based on the idea that all learners have four major styles which must be mastered in order to achieve balance (McCarthy, 1996, p. 201). The four styles are represented by a circle divided into four quadrants, through which the student cycles in order to learn successfully. The focus of Quadrant One is on personal meaning; Quadrant Two on expert knowledge; Quadrant Three on practical tinkering; and Quadrant Four on individual creativity. An equal number of opportunities to use both the right and the left sides of the brain expands the 4MAT four-phase system to eight steps. Once teachers are familiar with the phases, they are encouraged to design instruction with the 4MAT cycle as a base for lesson planning, teaching, and assessment. 4MAT can be used with kindergartners through adults.

An assessment tool has been developed to accompany the 4MAT method, entitled The Learning Type Measure (McCarthy, 1993). This assessment tool provides teachers with information about how learners best select, organize, represent, and process knowledge. Results of the student questionnaire are plotted on a four-quadrant graph to assist in easily interpreting learner strengths and weaknesses. (See Resources section for ordering information.)

Other Tools

Other well known instruments include the Gregorc Style Delineator (Gregorc, 1982) and the Myers-Briggs Type Indicator (1975). These assessment formats have been designed for adults rather than children and would not be appropriate for young children or adolescents.

In addition to these instruments, many schools and educators have developed their own learning style assessment tools. A recent search on the Internet identified a half dozen of these self-made questionnaires. Although these tools are convenient and free of charge, their reliability and validity are unknown.

Whether you use observation, standardized tests, or informal assessment tools, once you have gained a sense of each student's individual learning style, you can provide instruction and modifications that better match student needs.

Chapter 2

Teaching Your Students About Learning Styles

᷾

"Student-directed learning." "Engagement." "Constructivist learning." "Student empowerment." These phrases are frequently used in our schools, within mission statements, in staff development programs, and in hallway conversations. They reflect the philosophy that for learners to maximally benefit from their school experience, they must be actively involved and offered opportunities for reasonable control over their own learning. One way to accomplish active involvement is to teach students about their individual learning styles and preferences. Refer to **Figure 2.1** as an easy reference. With this information, students can begin to seek out and advocate for opportunities which match their styles.

What are the specific advantages to learners and teachers when students know and understand their own learning styles?

᷾ Students who know their own learning styles can make appropriate choices about learning activities. For example, when students have been asked to demonstrate their knowledge of the solar system, an auditory learner may be more successful in choosing to give an oral report, whereas a poster presentation may be more

beneficial for a tactile learner. Students who know their own learning strengths are able to select the instructional activities in which they can succeed.

᷾ Learners can advocate for appropriate accommodations. For example, a kinesthetic learner who needs frequent movement can negotiate with the classroom teacher for a standing workstation. This accommodation may then make it easier for a kinesthetic learner to succeed at a visual task such as a workbook page.

᷾ Students can proactively use coping strategies during instruction that does not match their learning style. For example, visual learners can use notetaking or symbols, or can imagine events while listening to a teacher lecture. By adding a visual component to auditory input, these visual learners will increase their retention of information.

᷾ All students benefit when they understand that a learning style *difference* is not a *failure*. Learning styles and other differences are a natural part of our human existence, to be embraced. Teachers can help students understand this by following the ideas in this book. It is fair and right for teachers to embrace and accommodate learning styles.

With all of these advantages, it makes sense to teach students about learning styles. Many ideas for teaching about learning styles and instructing through the four modalities are included in this book. As you incorporate these ideas into your instruction, be sure to share these important points with students:

❧ Everyone learns through all four modalities (visual, auditory, tactile, kinesthetic). However, most people learn through one modality more easily and quickly than through the other three.

❧ No single modality is better than the others. All four can be used to learn new information and express ideas.

❧ Teachers have learning style preferences just as students do. This may impact the way that they teach and organize their classrooms.

❧ By interacting with peers, students can learn other ways to approach learning. For example, auditory learners can ask visual learners about how they study and then incorporate some of the techniques into their own repertoire.

❧ It is fair for teachers to make adaptations for individual student learning styles so that all students learn successfully. This, of course, is the goal of education.

❧ All people experience times when instruction does not match their learning style, and must learn to cope by seeking and utilizing other learning strategies. For example, a tactile learner listening to a lecture on syllabication may cope by doodling, finger spelling, or tapping a related rhythm.

❧ There are appropriate times for students to advocate for themselves in regard to learning styles. By approaching teachers before or after class or during breaks and politely describing their needs, students are likely to find teachers ready and willing to collaborate.

To help all your students understand learning styles, be sure to design lessons which incorporate all four modalities. The **Tables 3** and **4** have been used to teach students about their learning styles. You may wish to choose one activity from each category and combine them into a single lesson, or use individual activities over the course of several days or weeks.

Learning Styles: General Concepts to Share With Students

❑ Everyone learns through all four modalities (visual, auditory, tactile, kinesthetic).

❑ No single modality is better than the others.

❑ Teachers have learning style preferences just as students do.

❑ By interacting with peers, students can learn other ways to approach learning.

❑ It is fair for teachers to make adaptations for individual student learning styles so that all students learn successfully.

❑ All people experience times when instruction does not match their learning style, and must learn to cope by seeking and utilizing other learning strategies.

❑ There are appropriate times for students to advocate for themselves in regard to learning style.

Figure 2.1

Table 3: Teaching Students About Learning Styles

Visual

- Provide a diagram of quadrants with examples (Table 2).
- Have students read books about styles (see Resources).
- Show pictures of different types of learning activities or have students draw examples.
- Draw symbols (ear, eye, fingers, body) for the four learning styles.
- Show a videotape of students engaged in different types of learning.

Auditory

- Listen to stories about learning styles (see Resources) read by teachers, parents, or other students.
- Listen to various styles of music, discuss individual preferences, and relate preferences to learning styles.
- Listen to books on tape about learning styles. (Create from books in Resources.)
- Practice quiet and loud classroom environments for approximately ten minutes and discuss preferences.
- Coordinate small groups of same-style learners for a discussion of learning styles, then re-group so that all four modalities are presented in each small group. Discuss again.

Tactile

- Have each student write his or her name and preferred style on a Post-it note. Then have students stick their Post-it notes to a board and group them according to the four styles. Discuss which are most common in the class.
- Using individual wipe-off boards, have students write learning preferences and hold above for all to see.
- Describe various activities on individual index cards. Then have students sort index cards by learning modality to see if they understand the differences.
- Ask students to respond to yes or no questions by making N and Y shapes with their fingers.

Kinesthetic

- Post four Wall Charts, one on each side of the classroom, and ask students to move to the section that represents their learning style.
- Develop a Hop-Step Mat indicating preferences (see Section 2). Students can step or hop to areas on the Mat that represent their styles.
- Ask students to stand and sit in response to questions about learning style.
- Have students step left or right in response to questions.
- Ask students to act out, silently or with words, specific learning styles.

Table 4: Teaching Students About Learning Styles

Visual

- Make bar graphs documenting class learning styles. Include the percentage of each day spent within each style.
- Have students write about learning situations in which they feel frustrated or successful.
- Create a list of fun, afterschool activities and categorize them according to learning modality.
- Present each learning style in a specific color on an overhead projector.

Auditory

- Have students interview family members about learning styles.
- Develop a mock radio commercial about learning styles.
- Write and sing songs about learning styles.
- Discuss times when students have felt frustrated or successful in a learning situation.
- Read aloud poetry about styles (see Resources).
- Ask students to develop oral stories about characters with specific learning styles.

Tactile

- Ask students to respond to questions about style using Yes or No index cards.
- Ask students to sit with their hands in their laps. Then provide each student with an object to hold or play with. Discuss how it feels to sit still versus touching and holding something.
- Ask students to bring in objects from home that represent their learning styles.
- Develop a felt board using symbols of learning styles.
- Using four puppets to represent the four modalities, have students put on a puppet show about learning styles.

Kinesthetic

- Ask students to stand in a circle and toss a ball. The student who catches the ball shares his or her learning style.
- Have students walk to a classroom area which is primarily for one type of learning style (e.g., Listening Centers are auditory, Math Manipulatives are tactile).
- Discuss student preferences of afterschool activities.
- Have all students stand as they work and then sit as they work. Discuss student preferences.
- Using sidewalk chalk, record information about student learning styles in the playground (e.g., pie chart showing learning preferences of the class).

Chapter 3

The Home-School Connection

$\mathcal{A}$ strong connection between home and school is important to ensure successful learning, but this connection is often difficult to make. While many parents take active roles as school volunteers, others are limited by work schedules and other responsibilities. Even though today's parents are very busy, they generally want to support their children's education. One way to build a connection and elicit parental support is to share the learning styles philosophy and information with parents.

By informing parents about the learning styles philosophy at your school you are helping them to understand how learning styles affect their children's school performance. You are also enabling parents to assist when their children become frustrated with school experiences, have difficulty choosing a project option to work on, or have questions about learning differences. This is especially critical for students who are experiencing great difficulty in school. These students need schoolwork and homework activities to match their styles, so as not to become frustrated and give-up.

Parents can provide effective homework support if they are kept informed. Nothing is more frustrating for parents,

students, and teachers than effort spent on homework that does not seem to pay off. Many times lack of progress in homework is due to parents approaching homework from their own learning styles, rather than from their children's learning styles. For example, the parent who is an auditory learner often relies on lengthy verbal instructions. This works well if the child is also an auditory learner. However, if the child is primarily a tactile learner, progress will be slow and frustration high. A sense*Able* approach to homework is to inform parents of the learning styles of their children and suggest strategies that correspond to learning style. This practice makes homework time a more efficient, effective time for parents and children to work together.

There are many ways to inform parents about learning styles. One of the most effective is through a Family Night workshop. A Family Night workshop is an event, usually held in the early evening, in which parents and children can learn together. These workshops send a clear message to students that parents are interested and informed about school activities, and wish to support their learning.

For a Family Night workshop on learning styles, parents and children can come together and experience station activities representing various learning styles. For example, participants might be taught to build a three-dimensional model by auditory input, visual input, tactile input, or kinesthetic input. Participants can complete reaction cards after each activity, reporting on how easy or difficult the task seemed. After participants have experienced the different styles, staff can lead small group discussions about how learning differences are addressed in the classroom. Parents can also fill out brief questionnaires to help them assess their own learning preferences. Finally, specific information can be provided on how parents can respond to their children's learning styles at home.

In addition to Family Night workshops, individual parent-teacher conferences can be wonderful vehicles for relaying information on learning styles. These meetings give parents the opportunity to ask specific questions about their children's learning styles and how they can help at home. To make the most efficient use of conference time, send parents information about learning styles in advance and encourage them to prepare questions for the conference.

If parents are unable to attend a Family Night workshop or a parent-teacher conference, written communication can inform parents about the learning style approach in your school. The following reproducible **Sample Letter to Parents** explains a school-based learning style initiative. The reproducible lists of learning style strategies (**Reproducibles C and D**) can be attached to the letter to parents. This information may spark enough interest that parents will seek a conference with the teacher to learn more.

$\mathcal{S}$ense*Able* Strategies

Dear

Recently, our faculty has been exploring the impact of individual learning styles on the educational process. We have identified student learning styles and have been incorporating this information into our teaching. Our success with this approach has been exciting and we wish to share it with you.

The phrase *learning styles* refers to a specific combination of factors which affect how easily and efficiently an individual is able to learn. These factors include: time of day, structure, lighting, temperature, and the way material is presented. It is this last factor, often called perceptual input, that our staff has found particularly helpful. As a parent, you play a key role in your child's learning and in practicing skills at home. Learning styles information can be of great help to you as you work with your child. Your child, _____, is primarily:

❑ **A Visual Learner.** A visual learner learns more easily when given things to look at. Reading, color highlighting, looking at pictures, outlining, and watching demonstrations aid visual learners.

❑ **An Auditory Learner.** An auditory learner learns more easily by listening. Rhythmic chants, lectures, stories on tape, and verbal directions aid auditory learners.

❑ **A Tactile Learner.** A tactile learner learns more easily by touching materials related to the learning. Arts and crafts projects, letter shapes made from pipe cleaners, finger-counting, and manipulating small objects aid tactile learners.

❑ **A Kinesthetic Learner.** A kinesthetic learner learns more easily by moving his or her body. Forming letter shapes with body parts, jumping out rhythms of multisyllable words, acting out meanings of words, and demonstrating activities aid kinesthetic learners.

Use the enclosed list of strategies when you work with your child on homework or other learning activities.

Please contact _____ if you have any questions or would like to know more about learning styles.

Sincerely,

Strategies for Helping Your Child at Home

Try these ideas with your child during homework time, when giving directions, or when teaching your child something new. Try several ideas. As each child is unique, some ideas will work better than others, so experiment and have fun!

If your child is a primarily visual learner, try one or more of these ideas:

- Use color highlighters to highlight words or directions.
- Demonstrate tasks for your child.
- Encourage your child to use colored markers or crayons for writing or math.
- Show your child graphic symbols or icons (such as those in a book or on a computer) when explaining concepts.
- Write down steps or directions for your child, or have your child write them.
- Encourage your child to outline the main ideas and supporting details when studying or reading.

If your child is primarily an auditory learner, try one or more of these ideas:

- Encourage your child to listen to words, stories, and music on audiotape.
- Help your child remember information by making up songs together.
- Encourage your child to repeat information out loud several times.
- Allow your child to listen to background instrumental music (e.g., classical) while studying.
- Have your child teach someone else the information being learned.
- Record the directions or steps of a task on an audiotape and have your child listen to it.

Strategies for Helping Your Child at Home

Try these ideas with your child during homework time, when giving directions, or when teaching your child something new. Try several ideas. As each child is unique, some ideas will work better than others, so experiment and have fun!

If your child is primarily a tactile learner, try one or more of these ideas:

- ❧ Encourage your child to use small objects as counters when doing addition and subtraction.
- ❧ Provide a small object to hold when your child needs to listen for long periods of time.
- ❧ Direct your child to trace letters, words, or symbols with a finger.
- ❧ Show your child how to "write it" in the air with his or her finger.
- ❧ Encourage your child to clap hands or snap fingers to the rhythm of the word or information being learned.

If your child is primarily a kinesthetic learner, try one or more of these ideas:

- ❧ Encourage your child to stand while working.
- ❧ Allow your child to take frequent exercise breaks.
- ❧ Role play with your child or have him/her act out information.
- ❧ Ask your child to step to the left to indicate yes as an answer, and to the right to indicate no as an answer.
- ❧ Take your child to explore places in the community which relate to the subject being learned.

Chapter 4

Lesson Planning

ॐ

Integrating learning styles into lesson planning need not be complicated or overwhelming. The simplest approach is to focus on one aspect of learning styles and begin to experiment. Many teachers find it best to start by thinking about the perceptual modalities (visual, auditory, tactile, and kinesthetic) as they plan the lesson. **Reproducible E** is divided into four parts—one for each modality. As you brainstorm, list ideas for accomplishing your lesson objectives in the appropriate area. List *all* your ideas, even those you don't think you will use—you may decide to use them at another time!

The following samples (**Figures 4.1, 4.2,** and **4.3**) show the results of brainstorming sessions for three lessons, incorporating all four modalities. As you look over the samples, try to recognize the strategies that might apply to your content objectives. There's no need to "reinvent the wheel" for each new lesson.

esson Plan

Subject:_____ Activity: _____

Lesson Objective: _____

Visual	**Auditory**
Tactile	**Kinesthetic**

*L*esson Plan

Subject: <u>Language Arts</u>   Activity: <u>Three-Paragraph Essay Writing</u>

Lesson Objective: <u>Students will write a three-paragraph essay with a clear beginning, middle, and end.</u>

Visual	**Auditory**
Highlight components. Use graphic organizers at desk/on overhead. Ask students to draw a Graphic Summary (see Section 2). Provide a written reminder of the main components of an essay on board or desk.	Listen to soft music in background (see Section 2, "Walkman Wonders"). Tape record verbal instructions. Repeat key concepts aloud as group. Read paragraphs aloud, recording them on tape. Then play them back.
Tactile	**Kinesthetic**
Provide students with index cards for writing (see Section 2, "Index Cards"). Provide objects to touch prior to writing about them. Use Wikki Stix to divide the sheet of paper into three sections, one for each paragraph (see Section 2, "Wikki Stix"). Design felt storyboards prior to writing.	Ask students to stand as they work at their desks (see Section 2, "Standing Workstations"). Have students stand/sit in response to questions (see Section 2, "Stand in Response"). Ask students to mime concepts before writing. Set up three stations in the room, one per paragraph, and have students move to the next station as they progress in their writing.

Figure 4.1: Sample Lesson Plan

$\mathcal{L}$esson Plan

Subject: __Math__   Activity: __Two-Digit Multiplication__

Lesson Objective: __Students will accurately compute two-digit multiplication problems.__

Visual

Provide examples on overhead transparencies.

Use a graphic organizer of math process.

Have students use colored pencils to draw columns on their papers.

Develop overlays on transparencies, using different colors to show each step.

Auditory

Talk through the math process before, during, and/or after problem-solving.

Provide students with headphones to block out noise as they work on problems.

Allow students to talk with a partner to solve problems.

Quiz students orally.

As a group, brainstorm methods to solve math problems.

Ask students to write rhymes or raps and then perform them.

Tactile

Provide students with manipulatives, such as plastic bottle caps, to solve problems.

Solve problems with magnetic numbers on a cookie sheet rather than on paper.

Use Magic Finger Writing to practice equations (see Section 2).

Use glue to draw column lines on paper. Let glue dry. These lines can now serve as column guides.

Kinesthetic

Step to numbers on Hop-Step Mat that correspond to correct solution (see Section 2).

Have students work out problems on the chalkboard or on chart paper.

Give cards with numbers to students and have them move to correct places to show the answer.

Figure 4.2: Sample Lesson Plan

$\mathcal{L}$esson Plan

Subject: <u>Language Arts</u>   Activity: <u>Identifying Nouns</u>

Lesson Objective: <u>Students will accurately identify words which are nouns versus those that are not.</u>

Visual

Circle nouns with red on overhead transparency.

Stick nouns to a Stick-to-Me Apron (see Section 2).

Give students Highlighting Tape to highlight nouns on a page (see Section 2).

Draw pictures of the nouns with colored markers or have students draw pictures.

Auditory

Have students clap once when noun is spoken aloud.

Use a noisemaker or bell each time a noun is used.

Have students whisper the nouns when reading aloud.

Help students develop and perform raps about the properties of nouns.

Tactile

Have students touch items that represent different types of nouns (e.g., cloth, books, pencils).

Have students clap out a rhyme about nouns.

Ask students to hold up an index card every time they hear a noun.

Kinesthetic

Have students place Post-It Notes on every noun in the classroom.

Ask students to balance (or hop) on their right legs everytime they hear a noun.

Ask students to lean left for nouns, right for nonexamples.

Have students "air write" the letter N with a finger every time they hear a noun.

Figure 4.3: Sample Lesson Plan

Chapter 5

Assessing What Your Students Have Learned

$\approx$

*A*t a recent workshop on learning styles, trainer Tina Butt (1997) provided a simple insight: "If students don't learn the way we teach, then we must teach the way they learn." Likewise, for assessment of student knowledge to be meaningful, we must assess in the ways students learn.

Fortunately, student assessment has changed significantly over the last five years. Today's assessment strategies are more authentic and curriculum-based. The days of test papers as the only measure of student growth are quickly being left behind. In their place, educators are using a wide variety of assessment methods, including work samples. Matching assessment style to learning style is just as critical as the methods used. When a kinesthetic learner has been taught through the kinesthetic modality, doesn't it make sense to assess the student's learning in a kinesthetic manner? The answer to this question is "Yes, except...". "Yes," because matching assessment style to learning style gives the best indication of student understanding. "Except," because students also need to be able to succeed in more traditional testing

methods (e.g., on the S.A.T.). The first situation requires the teacher to match assessment styles and learning styles, while the second situation requires the teacher to teach students how to adapt to testing situations that do not match their learning styles. Effective teachers plan both types of opportunities for students.

The assessment techniques in **Reproducible F** can be used to match learning styles with assessment styles. As you develop new assessment techniques for your students, consider the four modalities and add the new technique to the appropriate modality section. Then, when designing assessments for specific learning objectives, review the techniques and select one from each quadrant. For example, when assessing student learning of rules for capitalization, a teacher might offer students the following options:

- $\approx$ Paper and pencil test (Visual)

- $\approx$ Oral questions and answer (Auditory)

- $\approx$ Develop board game (Tactile)

- $\approx$ Work at board (Kinesthetic)

Assessment Methods

Visual

- ❑ Paper and pencil test
- ❑ Drawing
- ❑ Diagram of content
- ❑ Labels
- ❑ Written story
- ❑ Matching column
- ❑ Overhead presentation
- ❑ Outline of content
- ❑ Photo essay
- ❑ Journal Entry
- ❑ Illustrated book
- ❑ Slide show
- ❑ Computer program or product
- ❑ Letter to the editor
- ❑ Other: _____
  _____

Auditory

- ❑ Interview
- ❑ Lecture on topic
- ❑ Oral question & answer session
- ❑ Discussion
- ❑ Homemade audiotape or videotape
- ❑ Debate
- ❑ Panel member
- ❑ Oral report
- ❑ Chant or song
- ❑ Walking tour talk
- ❑ Radio advertisement
- ❑ Poetry
- ❑ Eulogy
- ❑ Storytelling
- ❑ Other: _____
  _____

Tactile

- ❑ Models
- ❑ Diorama
- ❑ Art project
- ❑ Storyboard
- ❑ Felt board
- ❑ Board game
- ❑ Manipulatives
- ❑ Puppet show
- ❑ Handmade puzzle
- ❑ Clay sculpture
- ❑ Lego project
- ❑ Computer project
- ❑ Hand signs
- ❑ Scrapbook
- ❑ Other: _____
  _____

Kinesthetic

- ❑ Demonstration
- ❑ Implementation activity
- ❑ Dramatization
- ❑ Role play
- ❑ Chalkboard work
- ❑ Community service
- ❑ Peers directed to demonstrate concept
- ❑ Dance or movement
- ❑ Running a business
- ❑ Walking tour
- ❑ Charades
- ❑ Costume of period
- ❑ TV newscast
- ❑ Large construction project
- ❑ Other: _____
  _____

Section 2:
The Sense*Able* Strategies

$\mathcal{N}$*ow for the fun part!* Teachers love to find a terrific new idea, a creative new spin on an old idea, or to be reminded of an "oldie but goodie." The remainder of this book is devoted to providing lots of these wonderful, sense*Able* strategies. These ideas come from classrooms all over the country, and so have been proven to be effective and practical where it counts — in the classroom. Whenever possible, credit has been given to the educators who contributed. However, so many of the ideas have been swapped, shared, and developed along the way that thanks belong to all educators who endeavor to creatively instruct the students in their care.

Sense*Able* strategies are almost always multisensory because most students benefit from receiving instruction through a variety of modalities. In addition, it is difficult to dissect instructional strategies into single modalities. For example, almost every strategy is augmented by verbal directions and reinforcement (i.e., auditory input) whether or not the primary focus is auditory. Unless students are blindfolded, every strategy also uses visual input. Therefore, while the strategies in this book have been grouped by dominant modality, most strategies are

multisensory and can cross over into other categories

To assist in finding cross-over strategies that match student strengths or needs, each strategy is accompanied by a graphic key indicating the *dominant* modalities represented. (Strategies which include verbal directions are not considered *dominant* auditory strategies.) The auditory and visual strategies chapters contain fewer ideas because most classroom teachers already teach to these modalities extensively. However, be sure to explore these new auditory and visual ideas as well.

A strategy which utilizes one modality (e.g., kinesthetic) will be accompanied by this key:

$$\begin{array}{c|c} V & A \\ \hline T & \boxed{K} \end{array}$$

A strategy which emphasizes more than one modality (e.g., visual and tactile) will be accompanied by this key:

Of course, most effective teachers take ideas and modify them to meet their own needs and style, so modalities may change from the original if they are revised. In these cases, add your own personal key to each strategy.

As you read through the strategies, you will notice that most have been written for use by the entire class or at least several students. Often it is easiest and most effective to incorporate multisensory strategies into the whole class instructional plan. However, a few of the strategies are best used by only the one or two students in the class who are most likely to benefit from them. In order to avoid having these students feel awkward or singled out, be sure to use the ideas in Chapter 2, "Teaching Your Students About Learning Styles," to teach your students that learning differences are natural.

Chapter 6

Visual Strategies

High Contrast Backgrounds

Off-task behavior is a common problem in classrooms, especially when students are expected to do book or paperwork at their desks. While there are many factors that can lead to off-task behavior, one factor is learning style. Visual learners may be distracted by classroom noises or by the wide array of posters and visual materials around them. Students who are predominately tactile, kinesthetic, or auditory learners are frequently challenged by the need to visually attend to paperwork. High Contrast Backgrounds provide extra visual stimulus to draw attention to the work area, often resulting in an increase in on-task behavior.

Recommended Grades: K - 5

How To

1. Obtain large sheets (approximately 12-by-18 inches) of pastel, black, and neon colored paper. Black and neon papers provide a High Contrast Background to books and work papers. Some students have more success with black, others with the neon colors.

2. Ask students to cover their desks or work surfaces with the High Contrast Background paper.

3. Monitor students' ability to focus on their work and have students switch high contrast papers until optimum performance is attained.

More Ideas

  ❧ Cut 2-inch-wide strips of High Contrast Background paper and tape them around the top edges of the desk. This provides a simple outline for students who may be overwhelmed by a cover over their entire desks.

  ❧ Neon masking tape (available at many hardware and office supply stores) can be used instead of paper to outline the desk.

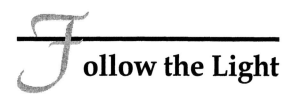 **ollow the Light**

Brain researchers tell us that our brains respond best to novel stimuli. Novelty causes the brain to develop stronger neuronal connections and to reallocate nerve cells to new areas. This strategy, Follow the Light, provides students with a novel tool to help them with the common task of reading lengthy material. By adding novel stimuli, students are more likely to remember the content and skills learned. In addition, the focused light source used in this strategy helps students sustain attention to detail in reading material.

Recommended Grades: 1 - 4

How To

1. Obtain several penlights or small flashlights from an office supply store or from companies that give them away as marketing tools.

2. Place the penlights in a central location where students have easy access to them, or give them to specific students.

3. Show students how to use the penlights to follow along in the text while the words are being read aloud or while students are reading silently to themselves. The light helps students focus on each word, and also keeps their hands from covering the words.

4. Have students practice using the penlights and monitor their use until you are sure they are using the penlights correctly.

More Ideas

Students may also use penlights to locate and highlight key vocabulary words, the directions on a worksheet, or parts of speech.

Source: Linda Tilton, Education Consultant and Trainer

hoto Reminders

Constantly reminding students of rules, behaviors, and expectations can become frustrating, especially when many students do not even seem to hear you. Visual learners often respond better to visual reminders of expectations. Photo Reminders, photos of students behaving appropriately, are taped to the corner of the student's desk. These then serve as a fun visual cue and are proof of the student's ability to follow rules.

Recommended Grades: Pre-K - 5

How To

1. Determine the specific, observable behavior the student needs to improve.

2. Ask the student to demonstrate the specific behavior. Then take a photograph. (Instant cameras are the most effective reinforcement, but any camera will do.)

3. Find a good location to post the developed photo. This may be on the corner of a student's desk, on top of a table, on a nearby bulletin board, or on a notebook or clipboard the student uses frequently.

4. When the student demonstrates an unacceptable behavior, walk over to the student, quietly point to the Photo Reminder, and then move away.

5. Depending on the needs of individual students, contracts may be set up and coupled with verbal reinforcement. Monitoring and collecting data on the frequency of specific behaviors is another positive strategy that can be used in conjunction with Photo Reminders.

More Ideas

As a whole class strategy, a bulletin board can be designed around Photo Reminders. Ask students to model the various behaviors expected in class. These may include: raising hands, standing in a straight line, sitting properly in their seats, sharing materials, and cleaning up. Photograph each student correctly performing at least one behavior, then post the photos.

Conversation Books

Today's teachers recognize that many children enter school lacking the basic skills required for developing friendships. As a result, many social skill and conflict resolution programs are becoming an integral part of school curricula. One important friendship skill is often overlooked in these curricula—the ability to find common interests. Conversation Books are small books containing pictures representing interests and activities. These books are strong visual tools that assist students in establishing commonalities with peers by providing a picture cue as a conversation starter.

Recommended Grades: Pre-K - 4

How To

1. Provide each student with a small photo album.

2. As a homework assignment, ask students to bring in photos, pictures cut from magazines, or hand drawn artwork representing aspects of their home lives and communities. Examples include: photos of family members and pets, pictures of hobbies, vacations, outdoor play, homes, yards, etc.

3. Encourage older students to label their pictures with words, phrases, or sentences.

4. Show students how to insert their photos and labels into the photo albums.

5. Throughout the month during appropriate times (e.g., indoor recess or at the end of a lesson), direct students to show their Conversation Books to each other. This may be done several times in the first month of school and less frequently during the rest of the year.

6. Model ways in which conversations may be started and expanded from a photo. For example:

    ❧ "You like baseball? So do I..."

     ◈ "Where was that picture taken?"

     ◈ "I have a dog, too. What's your dog's name?"

     ◈ "Who is that? Want to see my mom?"

More Ideas

If photo albums are unobtainable, Conversation Books can be made from construction paper. Substitute pictures cut from magazines, computer clipart, or hand drawn pictures for photographs.

ook Lights

Research indicates that young children generally prefer low-level lighting. Book Lights can be used with low lighting or with typical lighting to provide a visual cue for students to focus on their work. Book Lights are attached to books or clipboards, their light directed to the work area. This strategy is especially effective for students who are easily distracted from the work in front of them or students who prefer extra visual input.

Recommended Grades: 2 - 6

How To

1. Battery-powered Book Lights are available at many bookstores. You might also consider asking parents to donate Book Lights they are not using.

2. Show students how to attach Book Lights to their books. If magazines, workbooks, or worksheets are being used, place them on a clipboard and attach the Book Light to the clipboard.

3. Focus the beam of light onto the work area. If necessary, show students how to adjust the light to focus on different sections of the page.

4. Monitor to ensure that the light assists students and increases time on task.

More Ideas

- ❧ If Book Lights are not available, try letting students use small flashlights.

- ❧ Turn the lights off in the classroom and let students use the Book Lights to highlight their work.

- ❧ Allow students using Book Lights to sit on the floor under tables while reading so the beam of light is brighter.

Chapter 7

Tactile Strategies

ortune Tellers

Fortune Tellers have had a presence in classrooms for decades. However, only recently have they been used by teachers as well as students. Fortune Tellers involve the tactile and visual senses and can be used across the content areas. They are also a motivating addition to behavior management systems because students consider them fun. Fortune Tellers, folded paper devices which can be moved to reveal inside information, provide tactile learners with an intensive hands-on experience that can be linked to almost any subject area.

Recommended Grades: 2 - 6

How To

1. Pair-up all the students so everyone has a partner.

2. Have each student make a Fortune Teller using **Reproducibles G, H, and I.** (If working with very young students, provide each with a pre-made Fortune Teller.)

3. Ask each student to review the material to be learned and generate eight content questions and answers. Math facts, science vocabulary, spelling words, and other brief materials work well with Fortune Tellers.

4. Direct students to write their questions on the flaps labeled "Q."

5. On the "A" flaps, students write the corresponding answers.

6. When all the students have completed their Fortune Tellers, ask them to work with their partners. Students use the Fortune Tellers to question each other and check answers.

7. To use the Fortune Teller in pairs, Student A holds the Fortune Teller, while Student B chooses a number from 1-4. Student A opens the Fortune Teller that number of times. Student B then chooses one of the questions that are showing and Student A attempts to answer it correctly. The answer is checked by looking under the question flap. Students now switch roles.

More Ideas

Fortune Tellers can also be used in conjunction with reward or motivational systems. Select eight reinforcers which may be earned by students for good behavior, task completion, etc. Reinforcers might include:

- Bonus points

- Sitting at the teacher's desk

- Writing with a special pen

- No homework

- Computer time

- An achievement certificate

- Stickers

Reinforcers are written on the "A" flaps of the Fortune Teller. Color each of the numbered flaps a color. On the "Q" flaps, write another number. Use the Fortune Teller to reward a student by asking the student to pick a color, then a number, and give the corresponding reinforcer.

Fortune Teller

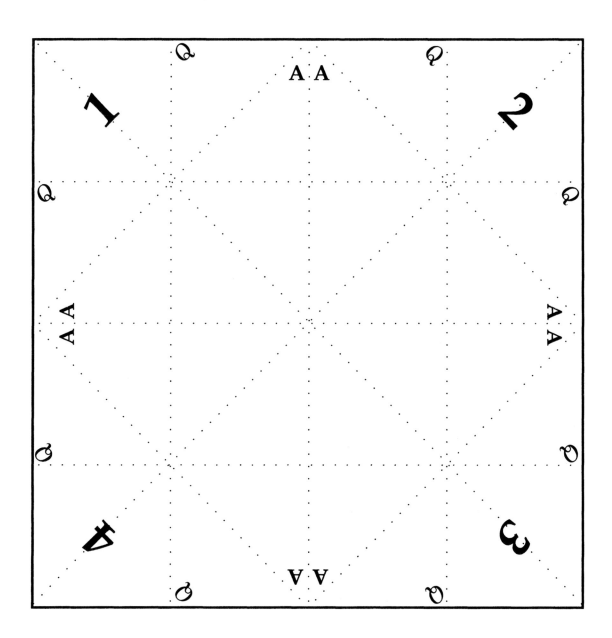

Adapted from *Teaching Friendship Skills* with permission. © 1993 by Pat Huggins. Available from Sopris West: Longmont, CO. (800) 547-6747.

olding the Fortune Teller

Directions: Follow the steps below to fold the Fortune Teller.

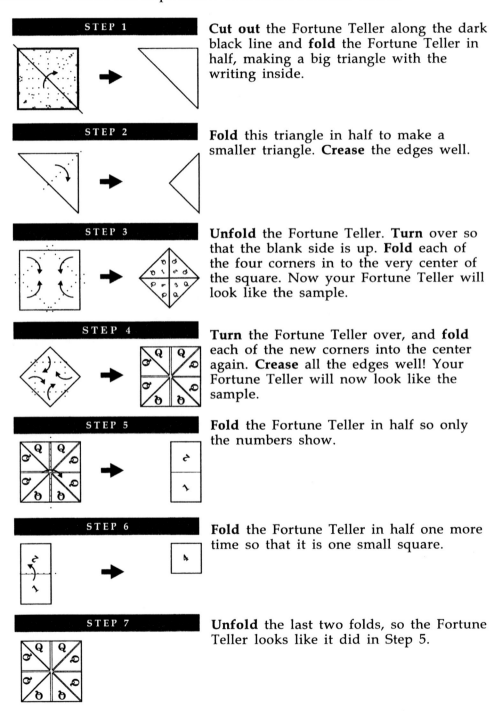

STEP 1

Cut out the Fortune Teller along the dark black line and **fold** the Fortune Teller in half, making a big triangle with the writing inside.

STEP 2

Fold this triangle in half to make a smaller triangle. **Crease** the edges well.

STEP 3

Unfold the Fortune Teller. **Turn** over so that the blank side is up. **Fold** each of the four corners in to the very center of the square. Now your Fortune Teller will look like the sample.

STEP 4

Turn the Fortune Teller over, and **fold** each of the new corners into the center again. **Crease** all the edges well! Your Fortune Teller will now look like the sample.

STEP 5

Fold the Fortune Teller in half so only the numbers show.

STEP 6

Fold the Fortune Teller in half one more time so that it is one small square.

STEP 7

Unfold the last two folds, so the Fortune Teller looks like it did in Step 5.

Adapted from *Teaching Friendship Skills* with permission. © 1993 by Pat Huggins. Available from Sopris West. (800) 547-6747.

Working the Fortune Teller

1. Stick your left thumb in the #1 pocket and your two fingers next to it in the #2 pocket.

2. Stick your right thumb in the #3 pocket and your two fingers next to it in the #4 pocket. As you do this, raise the flaps with the numbers on them so that it looks like this:

3. Now you have something that looks like a paper flower. By moving your fingers and thumbs, you can open and close the Fortune Teller in two different directions:

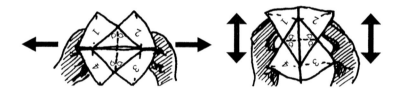

Using the Fortune Teller With a Partner

1. Hold the Fortune Teller completely closed and ask your partner to pick one of the numbers.

2. Open and close the Fortune Teller the number of times your partner picked. Alternate the direction you open the Fortune Teller each time. Leave the Fortune Teller open on the last count so that you can see the questions.

3. Ask your partner one of the questions showing in the open Fortune Teller.

4. After your partner gives the answer, open the flap in the inside of the Fortune Teller with the question on it. Was your partner's answer right?

5. Now its your partner's turn to use the Fortune Teller and you pick the number.

Adapted from *Teaching Friendship Skills* with permission. © 1993 by Pat Huggins. Available from Sopris West. (800) 547-6747.

 **ticky Labels**

Paper and pencil tasks can quickly become monotonous for all students. To add variety for tactile learners, consider using Sticky Labels during worksheet tasks. Words and numbers can be written on Sticky Labels first, then peeled and adhered to the correct space on the worksheet. Sticky Labels are also a wonderful adaptive tool for students with poor tactile and fine motor skills because they decrease time spent laboriously writing. Because labels are permanent, they also won't fall off papers prior to grading.

Recommended Grades: K - 6

How To

1. Obtain self-sticking mailing or file folder labels. Labels can be cut to the appropriate size for their use. The range is generally between ½-by-½ inches and 1-by-3 inches.

2. Have students write the words or numbers for the activity. (See "More Ideas.") For example, if students are doing a worksheet on verb tense, direct students to write several labels with "ed," several labels with "ing," and several labels with "s."

3. Ask students to peel the Sticky Label from the backing and adhere it to the correct location on the paper. For example, the label with "ed" would be adhered to the end of "play" in this sentence: Yesterday, I play _____ at the park.

4. If students' writing skills are very slow, illegible, or in other ways poor, then staff can prepare the labels for them.

More Ideas

The ways in which labels can be used is seemingly endless. Here are some ideas:

   ❧ Labels with student names can be used to head papers.

- Word choices can be written on labels and matched to a fill-in-the-blank worksheet.

- Single digits can be written on labels and combined for answers to math equations.

- Letters on labels can spell out words.

- Students can choose labels with correct spellings from groups that also include incorrect spellings.

- Vocabulary words can be matched to definitions.

- Coin amounts can be matched to appropriate coins.

- Digital times can be matched to a clock.

- Dates can be adhered to a timeline.

- State names or other geographic features can be adhered to a map.

- Single letters for initial or ending consonant sounds can be adhered next to a corresponding picture.

- Shape names can be matched to shapes.

- Color names can be matched to colors.

Sequence Heroes

Visual learners often excel in learning to use number lines, timelines, or other two-dimensional sequences, while learners who are not dominant in the visual modality may struggle. Adding a three-dimensional game figure, a "Sequence Hero," which can be slid along the number line, can enhance the attention and comprehension of students.

Recommended Grades: 1 - 5

How To

1. Good sources for game figures include tag sales and second-hand shops that sell previously owned children's games. Provide each student with a small game pieces to use as a Sequence Hero.

2. Help students choose storage places for their Sequence Heroes, such as in their pencil boxes.

3. When activities include sequences, direct students to take out their Sequence Heroes. Then show them how to manipulate their heroes in the sequence. Examples include:

   ~ Number lines on which students use their heroes to jump the numbers when counting or computing

   ~ Timelines on which students slide their Sequence Heroes to the correct point

   ~ Multistep, written directions on which students move their Sequence Heroes to the next step as each is performed

   ~ Daily schedules on which students move their Sequence Heroes as each activity begins

● Calendars on which students place their Sequence Heroes as they learn days of the week, dates, and other calendar skills

More Ideas

● Sequence Heroes can also be made by students from household materials, such as bottle caps, clothespins, Wikki Stix (see tactile strategy), pipe cleaners, popsicle sticks, or wooden ice cream spoons.

Source: Debra Jenkins, Oak Grove School, Cleveland, TN

ndex Cards

Students today handle hundreds of sheets of paper each week as hand-outs, pages of books, and worksheets. Because of this, students are accustomed to the texture and weight of most papers. An effective alternative for tactile learners is to use Index Cards. Index Cards are stiffer and heavier, providing fresh tactile input. In addition, more than one Index Card can be worked with at a time. Moving Index Cards around as tasks are performed provides even more tactile input.

Recommended Grades: 1 - 6

How To

Index Cards can be used in many ways. Try these ideas:

- Provide each student with two Index Cards. On one, have students write the word "no." On the other, have them write "yes." During question and answer instruction, direct students to answer questions by holding up one of their Index Cards. Ask closed-ended questions such as "Do you agree with me?" and "Is this the correct answer?"

- During writing assignments (in language arts, math, or other content areas) offer students opportunities to write on Index Cards instead of on typical paper.

- Hand out Index Cards to students and ask them to jot down key concepts or facts during class discussions. At the end of the discussion, ask students to post their cards on a bulletin board as a summary of the discussion.

- Use colored Index Cards to represent specific concepts. For example, students can be asked to write the main idea of stories on yellow Index Cards and supporting details on blue Index Cards. Math students may denote place value by color (pink Cards as hundreds, white Cards as tens, and green Cards as ones).

    ∾ Index Cards can also be helpful in self-monitoring. Students may keep Index Cards on the corner of their desks or tucked inside their notebooks. As they monitor their own behavior throughout the day, prompt students to make marks on the Index Cards.

Wet Writing

Wet Writing is a tactile, motivating activity that encourages greater speed in work completion. Students use a sponge-tipped applicator (such as an envelope sealer) or a sponge cut into one-inch squares to write with water on small individual chalkboards. This method may be coupled with standing at the board for kinesthetic input. Students find Wet Writing a fun, fast-paced experience that breaks up the sameness of the day.

Recommended Grades: K - 5

How To

1. If using an envelope sealer, fill with water and close tightly. The water will then keep the sponge damp. If using a cut kitchen sponge, provide students with a dipping cup of water.

2. Provide students with individual chalkboards or have them write at the chalkboard at the front of the room.

3. Explain to the class that Wet Writing is a game of trying to "beat the heat." The task is to write the answer or complete the math equation before what they write starts to evaporate. For example, to increase speed in spelling, say the word and have students use the sponge to spell out the complete word before the first letter begins to evaporate. To increase speed in math computation, provide a math problem and ask students to complete the problem before the first numerals of their answers begin to evaporate.

More Ideas

    Ș Encourage greater student participation by having students dictate words or problems to each other, taking turns with the Wet Writing.

❦ Wet Writing can also be used as an alternative penmanship process, without the focus on speed. For example, students who do not like to write, or who have poor letter formation, may benefit from this tactile approach.

❦ Try Wet Writing in other content areas. For example, students may draw an atom, put dates on a timeline, or trace the path of a ship on a map.

$\mathcal{F}$inger Feelers

Adult tactile learners can be found fiddling with paper clips, clicking pens, or touching jewelry. While these objects may be deemed appropriate to play with in the classroom, many others (e.g., paper wads, small toys, and keys) are not. Yet, tactile learners need tactile input and may demonstrate off-task behavior, disruption, or conflict without it. To help these students, try providing Finger Feelers for extra tactile stimulation. Finger Feelers are strips of fabric textures that students can quietly, unobtrusively run their fingers along during times, like teacher lecture, when they may not have opportunities for tactile input.

Recommended Grades: K - 4

How To

1. Collect a variety of fabrics. A wonderful source of fabric scraps is the local upholstery and drapery store. Fabrics used for home decorating are usually heavy duty, and scraps can be collected as items are made.

2. Allow students to sort through various fabric scraps and identify five fabrics they like to touch. Ideal fabrics include felt, velvet, and velour, or any fabric with a high degree of texture to it. Have students cut a 2-by-2-inch square from each of their five favorite fabrics.

3. Cut 12-by-3-inch strips of heavy duty fabric and glue them to the inside edges of students' desks. Make sure they are easily accessible.

4. Attach the small pieces of fabric students have chosen with Velcro to the base fabric, so that the positions may be changed occasionally.

5. At specific intervals throughout the day, encourage students to touch and rub their Finger Feelers, especially during primarily auditory instruction.

More Ideas

    ∾ If Velcro is not available, just glue the small fabric squares to the larger fabric base.

    ∾ For students who frequently work from a clipboard, consider attaching a miniature Finger Feeler to the top or bottom of the clipboard.

Source: Kimberly Porto, Teacher, Ridge Road School, North Haven, CT

Wikki Stix

Forming shapes, letters, and numbers with pipe cleaners helps tactile students learn. While pipe cleaners are fun, their sharp metal centers can be dangerous. A wonderful, versatile alternative to pipe cleaners are Wikki Stix. Wikki Stix are strings covered in wax. They are similar to candle wick but stick easily together so that long strands and larger shapes can be formed. Wikki Stix can also be stuck to textbook or workbook pages. By using Wikki Stix, visual activities such as reading and paper tasks are made more hands-on.

Recommended Grades: Pre-K - 6

How To

1. Provide each student with one or more Wikki Stix. Wikki Stix may be purchased at toy stores or teacher supply stores. (Also see the Resources section.) Students may keep Wikki Stix in a special place in their desk, or you may decide to keep a supply with other manipulatives in the classroom.

2. When introducing Wikki Stix to the class, allow students to experiment. Assign students to groups and ask them to brainstorm what can be made with Wikki Stix. Teacher favorites include:

   - Forming shapes

   - Forming letters

   - Forming numbers

   - Forming names or words

   - Using as bookmarks by inserting between pages

   - Measuring shapes and distances

- Underlining or circling key points in a text by pressing down until it sticks

- Underlining directions on a worksheet

- Using shorter lengths as counters

- Identifying colors (Wikki Stix come in a wide range of colors)

- Outlining an area to be colored by pressing Wikki Stix around the outer edges

- Making left and right margins on papers

- Marking travel routes and boundaries on maps

- Making lines on graphs

- Separating sections in a book or on a sheet of paper

3. Be sure to remind students that, as with all materials in school, if Wikki Stix are used inappropriately or become a distraction, they will be put away.

More Ideas

- Wikki Stix can be cut into shorter lengths if desired or can be used for measuring by cutting into specific lengths (e.g., 1 inch).

iddle-Stuff Basket

When tactile learners become nervous, excited, or stressed, they often manipulate objects in their environment. This produces a calming effect, providing an outlet for excess energy. Sometimes tactile learners pick unacceptable objects to manipulate such as toys, scissors, or keys. To prevent this, create a Fiddle-Stuff Basket. A Fiddle-Stuff Basket is a small basket containing textured, acceptable objects. Students are allowed, at times, to choose an item to fiddle with. This proactive strategy provides students with positive tactile stimulus during auditory or visual activities such as lecture or watching a videotape. Because of the tactile input, students will be better able to maintain attention.

Recommended Grades: K - 5

How To

1. Obtain a small basket, shoe box, or a similar container.

2. Collect textured objects for the basket. These may include Koosh balls, Thera-Putty, clay, tennis balls, porcupine balls. Any object that provides interesting tactile input without making noise can be put in the basket. Party goods stores and toy stores are excellent sources.

3. Fiddle-Stuff Baskets can be used in a variety of ways. For some students open access is appropriate. Students can then go to the Fiddle-Stuff Basket whenever they feel the need for a stress reduction object. Other students might have difficulty in determining appropriate times to go to the basket. These students might be offered the Fiddle-Stuff Basket when it seems warranted. Either way, design and review rules so that it is clear to students that the Fiddle Stuff will be taken away if they become distracted from learning.

More Ideas

> ❧ Ask students to brainstorm a list of objects that might be included in the Fiddle-Stuff Basket. As homework, send students on a scavenger hunt to bring in materials selected from the list.

Magic Finger Writing

Some activities can seem almost magical to students. Magic Finger Writing combines a feeling of "magic" with tactile and visual input. To perform Finger Writing, students use their index finger to trace words, numbers, or shapes that have been made with chalk. Then, using their "magic" finger, they can write on the chalkboard. The result is an effective method for teaching letter, number, and shape formation.

Recommended Grades: K - 2

How To

1. Use bright colored chalk to write the letter, number, or shape being learned.

2. Ask a student to come to the chalkboard and trace over the letter, number, or shape three times with the chalk. This leaves a thick base of chalk on the board.

3. Now ask the student to put the chalk down and trace over the letter with the index finger of his or her dominant hand. This leaves a thick residue of chalk on the student's fingertip.

4. Ask the student to write the letter, number, or shape next to the original model using his or her index finger covered in the chalk.

More Ideas

> &⋗ Finger Writing can also be used for spelling words or simple math equations. In these instances, have students trace the entire word or problem several times with chalk, and then repeat Steps 3 and 4, one letter or number at a time.

Source: Sue Allen, Casper, WY

Mix and Match Clothespins

Mix and Match Clothespins are a versatile way to involve tactile learners in matching activities. Key content concepts are attached to the backs of clothespins, which students then pin to the matching concept on a piece of oak tag. Mix and Match Clothespins provide strong tactile input, make abstract concepts more concrete, and are effective for developing the pincer grasp.

Recommended Grades: Pre-K - 3

How To

1. Obtain several dozen wooden or plastic clothespins. Supermarkets and hardware stores often carry clothespins.

2. Find a piece of heavy duty cardboard or oak tag, approximately 8 ½-by-11 inches. Holding the cardboard with the 8 ½-inch side at the top, write a column of math problems.

3. With a fine-tip marker, write the answers to the problems on the flat top of the clothespin.

4. Direct students to match the clothespin answers to the correct math problem on the cardboard.

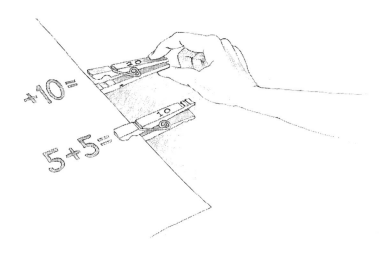

More Ideas

- Try using Mix and Match Clothespins with vocabulary and definitions, colors and color words, shapes and shape words, numerals and sets, coins and values, analog clocks and digital times, and other content areas.

- If you're hesitant to permanently write on the clothespins, write the answers on small pieces of paper and attach to the clothespin with a restickable adhesive such as Blu Tack or HoldIt.

Ticket to Recess

Listening to long periods of discussion can be difficult for many students, especially tactile learners. One simple strategy for increasing attention is the Ticket to Recess strategy. Students are provided with Tickets at the start of a lesson and are directed to write questions or statements about the lesson on their Tickets. Each student's Ticket is then traded in for access to recess. When used randomly, this strategy provides novel tactile input and increases motivation for all students.

Recommended Grades: 2 - 6

How To

1. Obtain a roll of large Tickets, usually available at teacher stores and office supply stores. As students settle in for the beginning of the lesson, walk around with the roll of Tickets and have each student rip one off.

2. Explain to the students that, for today, these Tickets will gain them admission to recess. To make the Tickets valid they must write their names on them and one thing they have learned about the topic. If students cannot think of anything they have learned, they may instead write a question about the topic.

3. A few minutes prior to recess, remind students about their Tickets.

4. Stand by the door as students head out, collecting Tickets as they go. If students have not prepared their Tickets, ask them to return to their seats and try again.

5. Read through the Tickets at a later time to find any questions students may have asked. Answer these questions as soon as possible.

More Ideas

    ↝ If a roll of Tickets is not available, use slips of colored paper or index cards.

    ↝ Primary students can write a single word instead of a concept.

Source: Adapted from a strategy by Larry Maheady, State University of New York, Fredonia, NY.

ice Games

Many students love to play Dice Games. The physical nature of rolling dice and the unpredictability of the outcome make Dice Games extremely motivating. Students who are tactile learners will especially benefit from the tactile input of shaking and handling the dice.

Recommended Grades: 1 - 5

How To

1. Obtain several sets of Dice. Larger dice are easier for young students to handle. If using Dice Games classwide, divide your class into pairs and obtain enough sets for each pair.

2. Direct students to take turns rolling the Dice. As the Dice land, one student uses the two numbers showing to form an addition problem (or subtraction, multiplication, or division). The student can write the problem on paper or use mental math. If he or she answers it correctly, a point is scored.

3. For more difficult math problems have students roll the Dice and combine the numbers to make a 2-, 3-, or 4-digit number (e.g., 516). Repeat two or more times until several multidigit numbers have been recorded. Next, use these numbers to develop math problems to solve.

More Ideas

ೠ Create Dice with the 26 letters of the alphabet. Roll the Alphabet Dice and make up words from the letters rolled.

ೠ Roll the Alphabet Dice and think of words that begins with the letters showing.

ೠ Roll the Alphabet Dice and make the sounds of the letters showing.

ೠ Roll the Alphabet Dice and find objects in the room that have those letters in their names.

ೠ Create Vocabulary Dice with new vocabulary words. Roll the Vocabulary Dice and make up a sentence including the vocabulary words.

ೠ Roll the Vocabulary Dice and define the words.

ೠ Create Dice with opposite words. Roll an Opposite Die and name the opposite of the word shown (e.g., big/small, up/down).

ೠ Create Color Dice, with either color words or actual colors on each side. Roll the Color Dice and name the colors or find them in the room.

ೠ Create Geography Dice with the name of a state, capitol, or country on each face. Roll the Geography Dice and locate the places on a map.

ೠ Create Dice for the parts of speech. Roll the Dice and think of words in the corresponding categories (e.g., adjective = strong).

ೠ Create Dice for any kind of categorizing. Roll the Dice and think of examples in the corresponding categories (e.g., mammal = cat).

ೠ To further increase the game element, design a simple game board on a piece of cardboard. Borrow game pieces from another game. When students roll the Dice and get the correct answer, they move their game pieces closer to the finish.

> **Adapting Your Dice**
>
> Learning activities with Dice can take many forms, especially if dice are adapted. To adapt Dice for the "More Ideas" uses, obtain sticky dots from an office supply store. White dots work best. Stick the dots over the faces of each Die and write the necessary letters or words on the dots.

Colorful Tile Chips

The best materials for tactile learners don't fade or disintegrate after a few uses. Tile Chips, available from tile and home stores, are fairly sturdy and can be used for many activities. They provide tactile learners with a concrete item to manipulate as they learn, thereby increasing comprehension and attention.

Recommended Grades: Pre-K - 2 (More Ideas are K-3.)

How To

1. Colorful Tile Chips can often be obtained from tile or home stores. Stores are often willing to donate extra chips or "seconds" to classroom teachers.

2. Place Tile Chips of various colors in a grab bag.

3. Hang specific colors of construction paper at various learning centers in the classroom (e.g., red at the drama center, green at the nature center, yellow at the writing center).

4. Have students reach into the grab bag and pick a Tile Chip. Then students walk to the center with the color paper that matches their tiles. Students do the activities found at the center until it is time to rotate to another center.

More Ideas

> ✿ Use GREEN, YELLOW, and RED Tile Chips during transition periods. Give each student one Tile Chip of each color to keep on their desks. Two of the three Chips should always be face down. When it's time to be quiet and listen to the teacher, students turn the RED Tile Chip face up. When it's time to get into groups, get materials ready, or otherwise prepare for an activity, students turn the RED Tile Chip face down and the YELLOW Tile Chip face up. When it's time to be fully engaged, students turn the YELLOW Tile Chip face down and the GREEN Tile Chip face up.

- Provide each student with a bag of mixed Tile Chips to sort according to color, size, pattern, or other characteristics.

- This idea might also be used with third-graders. Tile Chips are excellent props for measuring activities. Ask students to estimate how many Tile Chips are needed to fill the area of a 4-by-4-inch square. Then have them check their answers using the Tile Chips on graph paper. Students could also measure the length of objects by tile widths.

- Tile Chips make excellent manipulatives for counting activities. They provide a concrete way of making sets and doing simple addition and subtraction.

dapted Tile Chips

Tile Chips provide tactile learners with concrete items to hold and manipulate while learning or practicing. To increase their versatility, Tile Chips can be adapted for use by covering them with paper, labels, or stickers. Once adapted this way, Tile Chips can be used in a variety of content areas.

Recommended Grades: 1 - 5

How To

1. Obtain Tile Chips from tile or home stores. On one side of the Tile Chip, adhere clip art, symbols, or pictures. On the reverse side, adhere the word associated with the symbol. For example, one side would show a picture of a cat, while the opposite side would show the word cat.

2. Students place the Tile Chips on their desks with the words face up. A student reads the word, then turns the Tile to check his or her accuracy. This allows students the ability to practice independently.

More Ideas

- Adhere numbers and mathematics symbols to the Tile Chips. Show students how to develop and solve math problems using the tiles.

- Tile Chips can be used for discussions about emotions. Adhere pictures of faces with emotions (happy, sad, angry) to the Tiles. Ask students to pick one and think of a time when someone might feel that way.

- Spelling and vocabulary words can be adhered to tiles. Students pick tiles and form sentences or stories with the words. This activity may be done orally or in writing, in groups or individually.

- Lessons involving tables of information lend themselves to the use of Tile Chips. For example, Tile Chips can be adapted to show the scientific symbols for the table of elements. Students would be directed to place the elements (Tiles) in their proper place on a grid.

Source: Steve Harland, Oregon

Chapter 8

Kinesthetic Strategies

Stand in Response

This kinesthetic strategy can be used quickly and simply, without advance preparation or ensuing chaos. Rather than asking students to raise their hands, ask them to stand in response to questions. This involves the whole body in responding. Standing occasionally throughout the day also stimulates circulation and makes the mind more alert.

Recommended Grades: Pre-K - 6

How To

1. Throughout the day direct students to "Stand up if…"

    - "You agree with my opinion"

    - "You agree with Derek's answer"

    - "You believe that…"

    - "You know the answer"

    - "You have a question"

    - "You are finished with your work"

    - Content examples:

    - "You have traveled to another state"

    - "You were born in the summer"

    - "You know some sign language"

    - "You like to read science fiction"

    - "You have used a microscope before"

2. As soon as students have stood for a brief moment, direct them to sit down. Continue on with the lesson.

$\mathcal{S}$pinning

Strategies that are beneficial for kinesthetic learners are often beneficial for all learners. Spinning is a good example of this. Research indicates that Spinning helps the brain develop. Spinning also provides kinesthetic learners the whole body movement they need. Spinning can be incorporated into many classroom activities.

Some teachers may worry about Spinning being a distraction. Generally, students are intrigued and distracted by Spinning at first, but once it becomes part of the classroom routine most students no longer pay attention to peers who are Spinning quietly.

When Spinning is introduced to the class, most students want to spin. However, as the novelty wears off, many students stop Spinning. Those who benefit most (usually kinesthetic learners) will continue to request time for it.

Recommended Grades: Pre-K - 5

How To

1. At times throughout the day when students are reciting aloud, encourage them to stand and Spin in place as they recite. For example, students practicing the alphabet or math facts can stand up and Spin slowly and quietly beside their desks.

2. When students are reviewing the schedule for the day, reciting the seasons of the year, telling time, etc., encourage them to Spin in place as they are thinking, talking, or exploring these concepts.

3. Set some ground rules for Spinning. Rules may include:

    ❧ Spinning must be done quietly.

    ❧ No more than five Spins during a break.

    ❧ Spinning is done in a special place.

More Ideas

As a break, have students stand up and quickly Spin around three times, then sit down again. This break can be incorporated into any part of the day, as it is not content-related.

*H*op-Step Mat

The Hop-Step Mat can be used with all students and is especially beneficial for teaching kinesthetic learners. The Hop-Step Mat, a plastic shower curtain on which a grid has been drawn, is placed on the classroom floor. Students hop or step to the space on the curtain that corresponds to the teacher's direction. By using their whole body to respond, kinesthetic learners increase their attention and understanding.

Recommended Grades: Pre-K - 3

How To

1. Start with a white or pastel shower-curtain liner. These inexpensive, plastic liners can usually be found at grocery or department stores.

2. With a permanent marker, draw a five-by-five grid on the shower curtain, using the whole surface. (Make twenty-five boxes of equal size.)

3. Write one letter of the alphabet in each box, omitting X.

4. During language arts instruction, especially spelling or phonics, lay the Hop-Step Mat on the floor. When calling on students have them hop or step onto the correct letters to spell out words, indicate correct letter sounds, or spell out other answers. Encouraging students to call the letter aloud as they step to it will increase retention of the information.

More Ideas

    ∾ Make a Math Hop-Step Mat by dividing the shower curtain into a four-by-five grid, making twenty boxes. Write in the numbers 1-20, one per box. Then work with students on number recognition; addition or subtraction to 20; or other math activities, using the Hop-Step Mat as in the How To's.

  An activity that early childhood students especially enjoy is color recognition. Create a grid of four or more boxes and color each box a different primary color. Have students step onto the color box when learning color names.

  Use any of the Hop-Step Mats to enhance acquisition of a foreign language. Ask students to step to the letter, number, or color as you say its name in Spanish (French, Japanese, etc.).

$\mathcal{S}$tanding Workstations

Doctors tell us that when we are sitting, over two-thirds of our body weight rests on our lumbar region. While some students can tolerate this easily, many have difficulty staying in a sitting posture for any length of time. Kinesthetic learners usually leap at the chance to be out of their seats and move around. They actually *need* movement to *learn*. These are compelling reasons to consider implementing Standing Workstations.

Recommended Grades: Pre-K - 6

How To

1. Prepare an area in the classroom for Standing Workstations. Effective Standing Workstations provide hard, sturdy work surfaces at the appropriate height for students. If preparing more than one Standing Workstation, consider making them slightly different heights to accommodate more students. Workstations can be made from:

    - Drafting or architectural tables

    - Media or utility carts

    - Tops of a freestanding bookcases

    - Countertops

    - Varnished plywood or Formica can also be attached to a wall to fold up or out as needed

2. Determine rules for Standing Workstation behavior and communicate these clearly to students. Rules may need to address: wandering; talking; staying on task; and when, how, and by whom Workstations may be accessed.

3. Throughout the day direct students, especially kinesthetic learners, to go to a Standing Workstation. At the Workstation students may stand while they listen to a lecture, view a videotape, complete a worksheet, or read a book.

More Ideas

> ❧ Students generally perform very well at Standing Workstations, but sometimes wander a bit too far from the designated area. To correct this, outline a standing area on the floor with masking tape. Make it clear to students that they must stay within the lines or return to their seats.

Therapy Balls

Students who squirm, frequently leave their seats, and seem to be in "perpetual motion" are actually communicating. Their behavior is an indication of their need for more kinesthetic input. Therapy Balls, used as chairs in classrooms in Switzerland for many years, provide students with a more active form of sitting. Teachers report increased alertness, calmness, improved posture, academic improvement, and a decrease in inappropriate behaviors, from students sitting on Therapy Balls (Spaulding et al., 1998).

Recommended Grades: 1 - 6

How To

1. Obtain two or more Therapy Balls, one for the most active student, and another that can be rotated among the other students. For first graders, use 45-cm Therapy Balls. For second or third graders, 55-cm balls may be a better fit. Older students require larger sizes. Check with a physical therapist or physical education teacher for appropriate sizes. Therapy Balls are available from physical therapy supply stores and medical supply stores (also see Resources).

2. When distributing Therapy Balls, inform students that the balls are on a trial basis, and the privilege will be revoked if unsafe or inappropriate behavior is exhibited.

3. Demonstrate correct sitting postures and hang posters depicting correct posture as reminders. If possible, ask a physical therapist or physical education instructor to assist with the demonstration.

4. Discuss how to avoid damaging the Therapy Balls. Brainstorm with students to identify all the sharp items in the classroom to be kept away from the balls.

5. Monitor student use of the Therapy Balls carefully for the first few weeks, reminding students of correct posture and safety.

More Ideas

- ❧ Set up an exercise corner with Therapy Balls and a chart of exercises.

- ❧ Supply a therapy ball in a listening center for students to bounce gently and balance while listening to music or story tapes.

- ❧ Rotate balls in a predictable fashion around the classroom. Some teachers find that students like when balls are switched between the morning and afternoon.

Source: Anne Spaulding, Boulder, CO.

$\mathcal{B}$ungee Cords

Some students seem to have boundless energy. They move almost constantly in their seats, *when* they are in their seats. More often, they are walking or bouncing about the classroom. Allowing opportunities for active students to move frequently is helpful, but there are times when it is necessary for students to remain seated. At these times, it is often helpful to provide an outlet for their energy. One outlet uses a Bungee Cord. Bungee Cords are attached to the legs of students' desks. Students are then encouraged to bounce their feet against the cord. This will provide a great deal of kinesthetic input and decrease the students' need to move around the classroom.

Recommended Grades: 1 - 4

How To

1. Hook an 18-inch Bungee Cord (available from hardware stores) around the legs of the student's desk.

2. Adjust the cord so it is approximately 18 inches above the floor. Leave one side of the desk open for the student's chair.

3. To hold the Bungee Cords in place, wrap clay or a 12-inch length of masking tape around the legs, just below the hooks. Rubber stoppers, found in hardware stores, also work well. School custodians may have other helpful ideas.

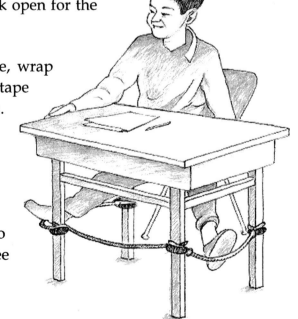

4. Periodically direct the student to bounce his or her feet on the Bungee Cords.

5. Monitor student use of Bungee Cords and adjust the height as necessary.

More Ideas

    ❧ Therabands can be used in place of Bungee Cords. Therabands are stretchy plastic strips often used in physical therapy or exercise classes. These can be purchased at fitness shops and medical supply stores.

Sign-Up Boards

No matter how small the class, there are always times when students have to wait for individual help. This waiting time has its difficulties. For example, when trying to assist one student, it is easy to be distracted by the line of students forming nearby. Students, especially kinesthetic learners, may also have great difficulty waiting quietly at their desks. In addition, much time that could be spent on other work is spent waiting for assistance. Sign-Up Boards, small boards on which students sign their names when they need help, decrease these problems. Sign-Up Boards give students the chance to communicate that they need help without interrupting. Sign-Up Boards also provide an opportunity for kinesthetic learners to incorporate acceptable movement into their day.

Recommended Grades: 1 - 6

How To

1. Designate a specific clipboard, small wipe-off board, or chalkboard as a Sign-Up Board. Label it for students.

2. Explain that when you are working with a small group or individual student, the other students should not interrupt. If students need help, they may walk to the Sign-Up Board and write their names under any other names.

3. Make sure that students understand that after they write their names on the Sign-Up Board they are to continue working. (Direct students to try the next problem on the page, begin work on the next worksheet, or take out a book to read.)

4. When finished helping one student, cross off that student's name on the Sign-Up Board prior to going on to the next student.

More Ideas

❧ Students from upper grades who serve as peer tutors in lower grades may also use the Sign-Up Board strategy. Peer tutors may assist students from the same Sign-Up Board or have their own.

$\mathcal{V}$oting With Your Feet

Rather than viewing students simply as recipients of information, effective teachers understand that students need to reflect, analyze, and evaluate information to make it meaningful in their lives. One method for achieving this is to have students consider other points of view and discuss whether they agree or disagree. Voting With Your Feet is a kinesthetic strategy which provides students with time to reflect and evaluate information being learned.

Recommended Grades: 1 - 6

How To

1. Explain to students that they will have the chance to show how they feel about something by Voting With Their Feet. When they agree with something, they should move to the Left. When they disagree, they should move to the Right. When they are unsure, they are to move to the Middle.

2. Direct students to stand up. Then say something like, "It's time to Vote With Your Feet. John's answer was _____. Where do you stand?" Remind students as necessary to move Left to show agreement, Right to show disagreement, and to the Middle if they are unsure.

3. Students can then return to their seats or vote on another issue.

4. Voting can be used in the following ways:

   - "I think you should work in pairs for this activity. Where do you stand?"

   - "This political candidate believes _____. Where do you stand?"

   - "Red is the best color for coloring fire. Where do you stand?"

   - "5 + 5 = 10. Where do you stand?"

   - "We should do our math work first. Where do you stand?"

- "It should be a classroom rule to never talk while a teacher is talking. Where do you stand?"

- "The North had good reasons for fighting the South. Where do you stand?"

- "Arguing is always a bad thing. Where do you stand?"

- "The best way to _____ is to _____. Where do you stand?"

More Ideas

- Rather than using a three-point scale (agree, disagree, unsure), try using a multipoint continuum (strongly agree, strongly disagree, and many points in between). Ask students to stand at a place along the continuum which they feel most accurately represents their opinion.

Chapter 9

Auditory Strategies

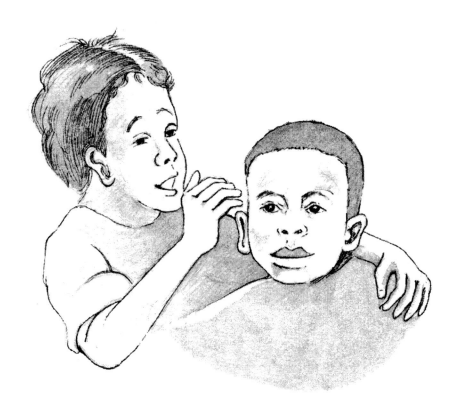

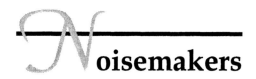 oisemakers

Auditory learners benefit from hearing a variety of sounds. A creative strategy for incorporating various sounds into the instructional day is the use of Noisemakers. Noisemakers are used to gain students' attention (and avoid straining the teacher's vocal chords!) In addition to providing novel auditory input for auditory learners, it is an effective strategy for grabbing the wandering attention of any student.

Recommended Grades: Pre-K - 6

How To

1. Obtain a variety of Noisemakers from a music store, party goods store, or toy store. It is critical to have at least three different Noisemakers, as students quickly learn to tune out sounds that become familiar. The novelty of the unexpected sound is the key to grabbing attention. These small, inexpensive Noisemakers are effective:

   - Harmonica

   - Slide whistle

   - Clapper

   - Shaker

   - Train whistle

   - Spoons

2. Instruct students that when they hear a Noisemaker, they are to quiet immediately and look at you.

3. Whenever it is necessary to gain student attention, play a Noisemaker.

More Ideas

• Link specific Noisemakers to specific requests. For example, use the harmonica to indicate that students have two minutes to finish an activity.

• When teaching students to self-monitor their behaviors, Noisemakers can be an effective cuing device. When students are to monitor their on-task behavior, cue them by shaking a rattle at random times throughout the day. When students hear the rattle, they make note of their behavior on a designated chart. Were they on task or off? (See the Resources section for books that include details of self-monitoring programs.)

riple Vocal Rehearse

Many adults learn things, like a new phone number, by repeating it aloud several times. Vocal rehearsing is an effective strategy for retention of new information, and it works with students just as well as it does with adults. It is a simple method for providing learners with auditory input, as well as recapturing the attention of students who stray off task.

Recommended Grades: Pre-K - 6

How To

1. Summarize a concept in a few words or use this strategy with simple, stand-alone information to be memorized, such as spelling words or definitions. After explaining the information to students, announce that it is time for the Triple Vocal Rehearse (or "Say It Three Times With Me").

2. Raise three fingers of either hand and encourage students, especially the tactile learners, to do the same. Announce the word or phrase to be repeated, then lead students in a choral response three times while raising or lowering fingers.

3. Use this strategy throughout the day, especially when student attention is waning.

More Ideas

    ∺ Encourage students to use the Triple Vocal Rehearse strategy at home when they are studying and memorizing information.

V	A
T	K

Reminder Messages

Many students have difficulty remembering to do tasks such as obtaining parent signatures, bringing back permission slips, or returning library books. Visual learners benefit from jotting reminder notes to themselves, but other learners don't always find this helpful. Auditory learners can increase their follow-through on tasks by utilizing the telephone answering machines found in most homes.

Recommended Grades: 1 - 6

How To

1. Create a list of student phone numbers and note those with answering machines.

2. Assist students in composing short Reminder Messages, for example:

    ❧ "I need to remember to bring in..."

    ❧ "Get Mom's signature on..."

    ❧ "Important! Remember..."

3. Once students have composed the Reminder Messages, they are ready to leave their messages. Take each student to a phone, assist in dialing if necessary, and cue him or her to leave the Reminder Message on the machine.

4. Monitor students for follow-through. Adjust the Reminder Messages as necessary.

More Ideas

   ❧ Students who have tape decks in their homes can record brief Reminder Messages on blank tapes during class and play them back at home.

Source: Adapted from an idea of Gretchen Goodman, Education Consultant and Trainer, Lancaster, PA.

alkman Wonders

While auditory learners are the most likely to succeed in traditional school environments, there are times when extra auditory strategies help students succeed. A Walkman, or small, personal cassette player with headphones, can provide a wide variety of auditory input. Students, especially auditory learners, are encouraged to listen to stories, math facts or other content through their headphones. This focused auditory input helps students comprehend, memorize and retain information more effectively.

Recommended Grades: 1 - 6 (More Ideas are K-6.)

How To

1. Obtain one or more Walkmans and blank tapes. Blank tapes that are shorter than 30 minutes are easier for students to rewind and fast-forward to find the beginning of the material. (See Resources.)

2. Direct students, particularly auditory learners, to retrieve Walkmans from the listening center.

3. Have students record their content onto a tape. For example, students may record the week's spelling words by reading aloud each word, its correct spelling, and reading the word again ("color," "c-o-l-o-r," "color").

4. After recording all of the spelling words (or other content), students can listen to their tapes over and over again until the words have been memorized.

More Ideas

- ✍ Give parents a list of upcoming stories to be read in school and ask them to tape themselves reading one aloud. Students love to hear their own parents' voices during school!

- ✍ Have students record themselves reading books and then listen to the tape of themselves. Students love hearing their own voices, too!

- Allow students to listen to select music while doing seat work. Research has shown that listening to specific classical compositions (such as Mozart's Piano Sonata in D major) improves spatial-temporal reasoning (Jensen, 1997, p. 20). (See Resources.)

- Students also benefit from wearing headphones by themselves. Headphones help block distracting noises while not blocking out teacher instruction.

- When giving lengthy directions, record them and encourage students to listen a second time, if they have questions. For example, directions for a multiday project (timelines, materials, expectations, resources, etc.) can be listened to repeatedly as the project progresses.

- Encourage students to tape themselves reciting math facts and to play them back.

- Students can record new vocabulary words and definitions or other memorization activities. These tapes can be used in school or taken home for practice.

- The Carbo Recorded-Book Method has been proven effective in helping students of any age learn to read and improve reading skills. These recordings are paced slower than usual and utilize a limited amount of material, so a successful reading experience is easier for students to obtain. (See Resources.)

- Students can break into small learning groups or work individually to develop and tape "commercials," songs, or news reports about specific topics.

- Students can develop raps, songs, or chants to help them memorize new information. Creating and taping these raps is a wonderful task for students in upper grades or students who have already mastered the content. As a creative writing task, students might also develop raps for younger students to listen to.

Chapter 10

Multisensory Strategies

Transition Cups

Transition times can be especially confusing for students working in small groups. Students are often so involved in working with each other that they have difficulty disengaging when it is time to stop, listen to the teacher, get out materials or put them away, or when it is time to start new work. Transition Cups are a visual and tactile signal for students, indicating each phase of a transition in a concrete way.

Recommended Grades: 1 - 6

How To

1. Obtain plastic cups in RED, YELLOW, and GREEN.

2. Make stacks of cups. Each stack contains three cups—one of each color (RED, YELLOW, GREEN).

3. Provide each small group of students with a stack and instruct them to place it in the center of their desk cluster.

4. When it is time to stop an activity and for students to pay attention, direct a student (preferably a tactile learner) in each group to place the RED cup on top. Describe to the students that RED means "Stop and look at me."

5. When it is time for students to get ready for work, put away materials, or follow other transition directives, ask a student in each group to place the YELLOW cup on top. Describe to students that YELLOW means "getting ready."

6. When it is time for students to focus on the assignment, direct a student in each group to place the GREEN cup on top. Describe to students that GREEN means "busy working now."

More Ideas

- ❧ To increase the likelihood of success, keep a stack of cups at the front of the room. At each transition phase, direct students to switch the cups while switching your own.

elcro Reinforcement Chart

Checks and gold stars work as positive reinforcement for many students but are usually less appealing to tactile learners. Velcro Reinforcement Charts, small cards designed so that Velcro pieces can be attached, provide tactile learners with more concrete input. Velcro Reinforcement Charts also provide a variety of visual input through color and high contrast, thereby appealing to tactile and visual learners.

Recommended Grades: K - 3

How To

1. Create a Reinforcement Chart for each student by adhering a 1-by-5-inch strip of black or white hook Velcro to a three-by-five-inch index card, a piece of cardboard, or directly to the desktop.

2. Using loop Velcro of contrasting colors, cut star shapes, squares, circles, and other shapes (each approximately one inch).

3. On the squares and circles draw "smiley faces," "WOW!" and other motivational messages using permanent markers.

4. When students behave appropriately or achieve in some area, reinforce them by providing Velcro reinforcers to stick to their charts.

More Ideas

   ❧ If you find that some students continuously pull the reinforcers off the chart (usually to hear the sound), this may not be the best strategy to use. As an alternative, try a felt strip with colored felt reinforcers that stick on top.

Magic Covers

Reading a text or storybook is often challenging for tactile learners and struggling readers. As a result, during "book time" students may become inattentive, frustrated, fidgety, or disruptive. Magic Covers are wonderful tools for decreasing these problems and for increasing student interaction with texts. Magic Covers are clear acetate report covers which can be placed over pages in a book. Teachers and students can then use colored markers to mark on the cover, as if they were marking in the book.

Recommended Grades: 1 - 6

How To

1. Acquire clear acetate report covers (Magic Covers) for each student and remove the plastic side clips (these will not be used). Magic Covers can be purchased wherever school supplies are sold.

2. Place a Magic Cover over the textbook page to be read, so that it covers the front and back of the page. This will keep the Magic Cover solidly in place. If reviewing several pages of text, you may wish to insert several Magic Covers at the same time.

3. The Magic Covers can now be marked with transparency markers, grease pencils, or other wipe-off writing implements. Mark the Magic Covers as students are working by:

    &- Highlighting the directions

    &- Crossing out some of the problems

    &- Changing subtraction signs to addition signs

    &- Circling new vocabulary words

    &- Drawing an arrow at the starting place

    &- Drawing lines dividing the page into thirds

4. Ask students to mark their own Magic Covers by:

    ∾ Doing math computation on the page, rather than recopying problems

    ∾ Circling all the words that contain a long "e" sound

    ∾ Underlining unknown vocabulary words

    ∾ Marking off page sections as they are completed

    ∾ Tracing the route on a map

    ∾ Circling important dates

    ∾ Writing directions or questions on the page

5. When finished, wipe the Magic Covers clean with damp tissues.

More Ideas

    ∾ Magic Covers can be easily used for recording assessments and general record keeping. Information from Magic Covers can be preserved, posted, or sent home by photocopying the Magic Cover over the covered material.

Transition Wheel

Auditory learners may be quick to follow directions to "Put your pencils away," or "Get ready for…". Students with other dominant learning styles may have difficulty during these types of transition periods of the instructional day. A Transition Wheel is a visual and tactile tool that assists students in moving through the phases of a transition.

Recommended Grades: Pre-K - 6

How To

1. Using oak tag or cardboard, cut two equally sized circles, approximately fourteen inches in diameter.

2. Divide one of the circles into three equal "pie" pieces. Color one third red, one third green, and one third yellow.

3. Take the second circle and cut out one "pie" shaped piece, approximately one third of the circle.

4. Attach the two circles at the center with a fastener. Make sure the colored circle is underneath.

5. Post the Transition Wheel where it is visible to the entire class.

6. When it's time for the class to be quiet and listen, turn the wheel to RED. Explain to students that RED means "stop." When it is time for students to gather materials and get ready, turn the wheel to YELLOW. Explain to students that YELLOW means "get ready." When it is time for students to

begin working, either independently or with peers, turn the wheel to GREEN. Explain to students that GREEN means "busy working."

More Ideas

- ❧ Kinesthetic learners may benefit further from being chosen to walk up to the Transition Wheel and turn it for the class.

- ❧ Tactile learners may work best with their own small Transition Wheels (approximately four inches in diameter). These may be placed on the corner of their desks.

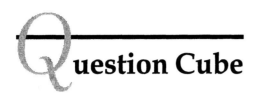
uestion Cube

Creating a game-like atmosphere during instruction increases the attentiveness of all students. Question Cubes, large handmade cubes with a question word on each face, are rolled by students. Students then generate questions about a just-read story. Particularly helpful for visual and tactile students who aren't as responsive to auditory input, Question Cubes draw on the visual and tactile modalities simultaneously, thereby gaining the interest, attention, and understanding of many students.

Recommended Grades: 1 - 6

How To

1. Begin by making a sturdy cardboard cube between 3 and 6 cubic inches. This can be done by cutting off the lower portions of two half-gallon juice cartons, washing and drying them, and then inserting one carton bottom upside down into the other, making a closed cube.

2. Cover the cube with self-adhering paper.

3. On each face of the cube write these question starters:

    &. Who?

    &. What?

    &. Why?

    &. How?

    &. Where?

    &. When?

4. During reading sessions choose students to roll the Question Cube and read aloud the question starter on top. Using the question starter, ask students to

develop questions about the material being read. For example, if the cube lands with "Who?" on top, students develop questions beginning with "Who."

5. After each student develops questions, the other students answer them. Then the Question Cube is rolled again.

More Ideas

- ❧ The Question Cube can be a whole group activity or adapted for use in small groups (each group with it's own Cube). It can also be used in pairs (each pair with a Cube) or used by individual students at home. To make smaller Question Cubes, follow the same method as in the How To's but use half-pint juice or milk cartons.

- ❧ To stimulate auditory learning, try enclosing a small bell or a handful of rice inside the Cube.

- ❧ Some teachers write poems on the Question Cube instead of question starters to help students memorize them.

- ❧ On each face of the Question Cube write subtraction, multiplication, and addition signs. Have students roll the Cube and develop math problems based on the sign on top. Students then trade their problems with other students for solving.

- ❧ Write sentence starters such as "Suddenly," "Thinking aloud," and "It really was. . ." on the Cube to help students extend their writing skills.

Source: Based on the work of Dr. Edward Gickling, Education Consultant, Centreville, VA.

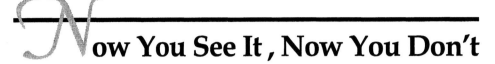

Now You See It , Now You Don't

Drill and practice are a necessary component of learning for all students. To add variety and multisensory input to these activities, try the Now You See It, Now You Don't strategy. This strategy employs red acetate as a cover for answer keys, allowing students to check their own work. By adding this visual and tactile twist to drill activities, student motivation and success can be increased.

Recommended Grades: 1 - 6

How To

1. Develop cards or worksheets with review questions or problems. Use a yellow or pink fine-tip highlighter to write in the answers on the cards or worksheets.

2. Cover the cards or worksheets with red acetate. You should now be able to see the questions, but not the answers.

3. Provide each student with a sheet of red acetate on top of the card or worksheet of questions.

4. Direct students to practice answering the questions, checking their answers by flipping the acetate back from the page.

More Ideas

     ↪ Encourage students and families to use this technique at home whenever reviewing material. Students may also develop their own answer keys, may bring one home from school to work with, or may develop answer keys with their parents' help.

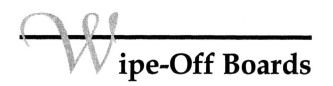

ipe-Off Boards

Wipe-Off Boards are wonderful tools for involving tactile and visual learners in recording their thoughts and answers. As an alternative to the reams of paper that students use every day, Wipe-Off Boards provide a stiff surface, allowing for writing implements that feel different from pencils and the use of a variety of colors. In addition, Wipe-Off Boards can be used in almost any subject area as an alternative to paper (e.g., spelling words, math facts, penmanship, vocabulary words).

Recommended Grades: K - 6

How To

1. Make Wipe-Off Boards by cutting sheets of 8 ½-by-11-inch oak tag or heavy construction paper. Laminate these sheets and cut away excess.

2. Obtain water-based, overhead-projector markers or wipe-off crayons at your local office supply store.

3. Provide a Wipe-Off Board and marker or crayon to each student. Direct students to complete their work on the Board.

4. For a permanent record, photocopy the Wipe-Off Board prior to wiping away the markings with a damp or dry tissue.

More Ideas

&» Wipe-Off Boards are a nice tool to use in cooperative learning groups. Provide each group with one Board and have one student use it to record their work. When called upon, students can raise their Wipe-Off Boards in the air so you can quickly scan their answers.

&» If Boards are available for each student in the class, they can be used for silent voting. After the students are given a choice (e.g., "Would you like math or spelling first today?"), they write their preference on the Wipe-Off Board and hold it in the air.

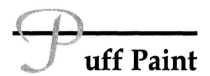uff Paint

Students spend so much time during the school day handling flat paper surfaces that they often no longer even notice them. Embellishing paper with Puff Paint is an easy, inexpensive way to increase tactile and visual input. By running their fingers across the paint ridges, students can feel the shapes formed. The bright colors draw attention to important points and can also be used to differentiate items on the page.

Recommended Grades: K - 4

How To

1. Puff Paint can be found at most craft stores. (It is frequently used for painting on T-shirts and fabrics.) Red and green paint are typically most useful, but varying the colors provides novelty and can broaden the applications.

2. Apply Puff Paint to the workbook pages of students who benefit from extra tactile and visual input. Keep in mind that Puff Paint can take up to ten minutes to dry. The less paint applied, the faster the drying time. Puff Paint is also designed to be permanent. It will stain fabric, so use caution and supervise students who are painting with it. Here are some ideas:

   ❧ Place a green dot of paint at the beginning of the directions.

   ❧ Place a green dot of paint at the beginning of the section to be completed by the student. Place a red dot at the end of the section.

   ❧ Place a red dot of paint below each number on a number line or chart.

   ❧ Place a green dot at the edge of the left margin and a red dot at the edge of the right margin.

   ❧ Paint a thin vertical line down each side margin of the paper, using green on one side and red on the other.

- Paint a thin vertical line between columns of multidigit arithmetic problems

- Color code worksheets to coordinate with subject areas (e.g., science is green, math is blue).

- Trace over numbers, letters, or shapes with a thin line of Puff Paint.

- Trace over trail routes or borders on a map.

More Ideas

- Encourage tactile and visual learners to incorporate Puff Paint into projects and reports they may be doing as homework.

Touch the Light Cards

Researchers tell us that combining two or more methods of sensory input significantly increases the likelihood of learning and retention. Touch the Light Cards combine visual and tactile input to support the learning of shapes, numbers, letters, and words. Touch the Light Cards are small cards on which a figure is drawn with marker and then emphasized with small holes along the figure's lines. When students hold the cards up to a light source, they see light shining through the holes. They can also feel the bumpy outline of the figure.

Recommended Grades: Pre-K - 3

How To

1. To help students learn to write their names, obtain enough index cards for each student in the class.

2. On each index card use a dark marker to write a student's name in print (or cursive for older students).

3. With a tack, poke holes along the lines you drew, pushing through from the back of the card to the front. This provides small bumps for students to trace with their fingers.

4. Show students how to hold the card up to a light source (a light box, window, lamp, overhead light) so that the light shines through the holes and provides a visual outline.

5. Direct students to run their fingers over the letters of their names.

More Ideas

- Touch the Light Cards can be made by students if they are old enough to use tacks safely, otherwise stick to making the sets of cards yourself.

- Develop a Touch the Light Card for each letter of the alphabet.

- Develop cards for the numbers 0-20.

- Make Touch the Light Cards for geometric shapes.

- Develop cards each week for new spelling words and place them in the spelling center.

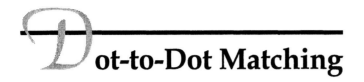

ot-to-Dot Matching

Many teachers encourage students to look through written materials to find answers to teacher-posed questions. The Dot-to-Dot Matching strategy provides visual and tactile input for students as they search for answers. In this strategy, questions are color-coded. When students find the answer to a question, they apply a dot of the same color to that section of the text or written material. Dot-to-Dot Matching is especially helpful for students who have difficulty writing out answers quickly or legibly.

Recommended Grades: 2 - 6

How To

1. Compile a list of questions. Next to each question, place a different colored dot. Dots can be drawn with markers or colored chalk, or marked with small, round adhesive labels.

2. Direct students to read the questions and locate the correct answers in the text. Next to the appropriate answer, students draw or place a small dot of the same color as the dot next to the question.

More Ideas

     ✎ Combine Dot-to-Dot Matching with Magic Covers (see visual/tactile strategy) when working in texts which cannot be marked on directly.

Source: Meg Mozdiez, Laker School, Wayland, MA.

aint Bags

Paint Bags are a simple way to combine visual and tactile input to reinforce learning of shapes, numbers, or letters. The colorful paint is also an appealing alternative to working repetitively with white paper and pencil.

Recommended Grades: K - 3

How To

1. Purchase good quality plastic bags with "zipper" closures. Small, sandwich-sized bags are best for single shapes, numbers, or letters.

2. Fill the bags with fingerpaint (approximately one and a half ounces).

3. Place the open bags on a flat surface and, with the edge of your hand, smooth out toward the opening so that air bubbles are released.

4. Seal the bags tightly and cover the four edges with double layers of clear tape.

5. Demonstrate for students how to form letters, shapes, or numbers by drawing on the bag with an index finger or with a blunt object such as an eraser. Then demonstrate how to "erase" the image by smoothing the surface with the edge of your hand.

6. When this activity is completed, pack away the Paint Bags in larger, sealed plastic bags or in a box, just in case a worn bag begins to leak.

More Ideas

❧ Mix two colors of paint in one Paint Bag and watch students have fun seeing the colors mix and change.

- Lay the Paint Bags on a light board to illuminate the letters more clearly.

- Use larger plastic bags for teaching words or math equations and fill with approximately three ounces of paint.

Content Puzzles

Puzzles appeal to a wide variety of ages and learners. An unfinished puzzle can quickly draw someone's attention and hold it until the puzzle is finally complete. This is especially so with visual and tactile learners who like to see and feel the pieces coming together. By using Content Puzzles, simple puzzles made from index cards, teachers can easily entice students to review and practice curriculum in a variety of content areas.

Recommended Grades: 2 - 6 (More Ideas are K - 6)

How To

1. Obtain index cards for each basic concept to be learned or reviewed.

2. On the left side of the card write one part of the material to be learned (e.g., the vocabulary word). On the right side write the matching part (e.g., the definition).

3. Cut the index card down the middle, creating jagged or curvy edges. For self-checking puzzles make each cut unique. For more challenging puzzles, make all cuts similar.

4. Separate the two halves and mix the puzzle pieces.

5. Direct students to put the puzzles together on their desktops or on a clear floor space.

More Ideas

In addition to vocabulary words, the following content works well for Content Puzzles:

- Math problem and solution

- Picture and label

- Shape and name

- Color and color name

- English word and foreign language equivalent

- State and Capitol city

- Food group and food item

- Abbreviation and complete word

- Analog clock face and digital time

ot Covers

For students who need extra visual input, Hot Covers provide an innovative method of cuing. Hot Covers are removable, self-sticking, transparent vinyl. They are available in neon colors on 13 ½-by-30-inch rolls and stick to almost any surface, but can be removed without damage. Teachers or students can cut Hot Covers into any shape or size and adhere them to textbook pages or worksheets. These Hot Cover cut-outs highlight key areas on the pages.

Recommended Grades: 1 - 6

How To

1. Hot Covers can be obtained at office supply stores (or see Resources for ordering information). Choose light colors that are easy to read through.

2. Cut the Hot Covers into various shapes for these purposes:

     ℓ Highlight a specific paragraph.

     ℓ Highlight a specific word.

     ℓ Highlight directions.

     ℓ Highlight questions at the end of a chapter.

     ℓ Highlight the main idea in a paragraph.

     ℓ Place bullets at important points.

     ℓ Place an arrow at a specific section of text or at a specific time period on a schedule.

     ℓ Place a star at the starting point.

     ℓ Place a green dot on the left and a red dot on the right to help students know where to start and stop.

     ℓ Place a red stop sign shape at the end.

- Place question marks next to paragraphs that contain answers to questions.

- Ask students to place question marks next to any material they have questions about.

More Ideas

- Of course, Hot Covers also make great book covers. Help students color code their materials by covering science materials in green, math materials in blue, etc.

- Color code reading levels of books. Cut dots of Hot Covers to stick on the cover of books as a visual cue for students. For example, students may choose a "red" book for independent reading or a "blue" book when reading with an adult.

ighlighting Tape

Highlighting Tape is reusable, transparent, and is available in neon colors. Visual learners who have difficulty with written material can use Highlighting Tape as a cue. Students who have difficulty learning in the visual modality also benefit from Highlighting Tape because it helps grab their attention and increases focus. Tactile learners benefit from extra input as they move the Highlighting Tape to different sections of their paper or textbook.

Recommended Grades: 1 - 6

How To

1.   Highlighting Tape can be purchased from office supply stores (or see Resources).

2.   Provide each student with a 5-by-8-inch index card and several lengths of Tape. Some lengths may be short for covering single words, others may be long enough to cover phrases, and still others may be quite long to cover lines of text.

3.   Have students stick the lengths of Tape to their index cards.

4.   When the class is working with text material (e.g., a science book), direct students to take out their Highlighting Tape index card. Throughout the lesson, direct students to:

  ❧ Highlight the directions.

  ❧ Highlight unknown vocabulary words (come back later to look them up).

  ❧ Highlight the sentence that answers a given question.

  ❧ Highlight the parts of speech in a sentence.

5.   Ask students to hold their books aloft so that you can scan the room and quickly find students who are having difficulty.

6. When finished, ask students to return the Highlighting Tape to their index cards for future use.

More Ideas

   ❧ Many students benefit from using Highlighting Tape while studying at home. Consider suggesting to parents that one or more rolls be purchased for home use, or provide several strips of tape to be kept at home.

V A
T K

raphic Summaries

Reviewing or summarizing learning is a critical aspect of an effective lesson. Many teachers review in an auditory manner, taking a few moments at the end of the lesson to highlight key points. While this benefits auditory learners, it is not as helpful for others. An effective review strategy for visual and tactile learners is to use Graphic Summaries. Graphic Summaries are simple drawings done by students to summarize key points learned in a lesson.

Recommended Grades: 2 - 6

How To

1. When approximately five minutes are left before the end of the lesson, direct students to get out their colored pencils, crayons, or markers.

2. Ask students to draw a simple picture, as quickly as possible, of one thing they have learned in the lesson. Show samples of simple graphics on the overhead projector. For example, at the end of a lesson on George Washington you might draw a row boat, a cherry tree, or an American flag.

3. Give students 30 seconds of thinking time to decide what they will draw, and approximately one minute to draw.

4. At the end of the drawing time, direct students to quickly show nearby students their pictures. If time permits, students may discuss their choices and drawings.

More Ideas

> ➢ Graphic Summaries can also be used in small learning groups. Follow the same steps, but have students work in groups with large sheets of paper. Make sure all group members draw something. When finished, post the Graphic Summaries and discuss. If short on time, discuss the Graphic Summaries as an introduction to the next lesson on the same topic.

ᘒ Lego can be used in a similar manner. Provide each small learning group with a handful of Lego blocks to build something representing their learning. It may be concrete or abstract in nature. Then have students describe their sculpture to the rest of the class. For record keeping purposes, take photos of the finished sculptures and their creators.

Picture Schedules

Although many teachers review the daily schedule with students orally, visual or tactile cues help learners who are not auditory-dominant understand what the day ahead will bring. By providing students with a Picture Schedule of activities, you help reduce student anxiety and increase responsiveness to transitions and timelines. Picture Schedules, chronological listings of the day's events, can provide visual-tactile learners with a clearer understanding of the day. As they progress through the day, students move a clip down their Picture Schedules to the next task or event.

Recommended Grades: Pre-K - 6

How To

1. Mark rows and columns on an 8 ½-by-11-inch sheet of thick paper, one row for each period of the day, and two columns—one column to write in the activity, the other for its picture. You might also decide to create a column for time notations.

2. Collect pictures or graphic symbols for each activity on the list, including special events. Pictures can be cut out from magazines, or may be photographs, computer clipart or original student work. Collecting pictures can also be an in-school or homework activity for the students.

3. At the beginning of the day, direct students to organize the pictures on the schedule in the proper order. This can be done with Velcro or restickable adhesive so that pictures can be reused and put in the correct order day after day.

4. Clip a plain or fancy paper clip onto the right side of the schedule, adjacent to the first activity.

5. At each point in the day when it is time to move on to the next activity, refer students to their Picture Schedules. Direct them to move the clip to the next activity.

More Ideas

- ❧ If the class runs on a fixed schedule, pictures can be permanently affixed to the paper.

- ❧ If students need assistance in organizing the schedule, consider assigning partners to review the schedule together.

- ❧ Older students may have less need for pictures on their schedules, but may still benefit from using a clip along the edge.

Source: Adapted from: Beninghof, A. (1993). *Ideas for Inclusion: The Classroom Teacher's Guide to Integrating Students with Severe Disabilities*. Longmont, CO: Sopris West.

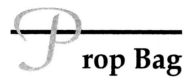
rop Bag

Recent brain research indicates that novelty stimulates the neuronal connections, validating what parents and teachers have always known: Surprises are the best attention-getters. Prop Bags provide novelty and surprise frequently without much effort. A Prop Bag is a drawstring bag which hides the objects to be used in the lesson. Prop Bags benefit visual learners by providing visual stimulus as the contents change with each use. Prop Bags also benefit tactile learners by providing concrete objects related to the lesson to hold, touch, and show.

Recommended Grades: Pre-K - 6

How To

1. Make or obtain a large, fabric, drawstring bag. If a drawstring bag is not available, colorful pillowcases can also work well. Just insert a drawstring at the open end so that the pillowcase can be tightly closed.

2. Brainstorm to identify items for the Prop Bag that illustrate what you will be teaching. The best props are usually small- to medium-sized objects that relate to lesson content. For example, props for an animal story might include:

    - Small stuffed animals

    - Illustrations or photographs

    - Habitat-related items, such as a bird's nest

    - Plastic animal figurines

    - Plastic people figurines (e.g., veterinarian, farmer, etc.)

3. Before students arrive for class, place the props you will use in the bag.

4. At the appropriate time in the lesson, pull out the Prop Bag. Build suspense by peeking in, asking students to guess, and shaking the bag. Then pull out the prop.

5. After showing the item to the class, pass it around the room, or ask tactile learners to hold it and show it to his or her peers.

More Ideas

&rm; If students in the class are in need of zipping or tying practice, try sewing a zipper or long laces onto the Prop Bag. Ask a student in need of fine motor skill practice to zip up the bag at the end of the Prop Bag lesson.

&rm; Rather than running yourself ragged finding props, try this. Announce upcoming units that will use the Prop Bag. As homework, students bring in objects that are related to the unit topic. Collect the objects and keep them under wraps until needed. This adaptation not only provides a simple way to gather objects, but also stimulates student thinking about the topic.

*M*agnetic Strips

Many primary students enjoy manipulating magnetic letters and numbers. Moving the magnetic letters and numbers around to form words and equations benefits tactile learners by providing concrete objects to manipulate. Unfortunately, magnetic letters and numbers disappear from the classroom as students move into the upper grades—and as the magnetic letters disappear, so do the tactile opportunities. Magnetic Strips benefit tactile and kinesthetic learners in the upper grades by offering the same opportunity to manipulate objects, while being more age-appropriate. Magnetic Strips can be used in all subject areas and can be beneficial for kinesthetic learners who may stand while using them on the side of metal file cabinets or on shelves.

Recommended Grades: 1 - 3 (More Ideas are 1 - 6)

How To

1. Magnetic Strip can usually be purchased at craft stores in a roll. One side of the Magnetic Strip is self-sticking adhesive, while the other side is magnetic.

2. Cut the Magnetic Strip into desired lengths, generally 1 - 2 inches.

3. On paper, cardboard, index cards, laminated paper, or other sturdy writing surfaces write the words from word families to be learned (cat, bat, sat; car, tar, bar) and stick them to the adhesive side of the Magnetic Strips. One to three students can work with each set at a time.

4. Have students place the Magnetic Strips on magnet boards, cookie sheets, or other metallic surfaces. Kinesthetic learners can use the Magnetic Strips while standing at metal filing cabinets or shelves.

5. Direct students to group the words from the same family together, then read them aloud.

More Ideas

Magnetic Strips can be used in a wide variety of content areas. Try these ideas:

- Equation signs (>, <, =)

- Vocabulary words and matching definitions

- Shapes of the fifty states

- Dates for timelines

- Capitol cities

- Shapes

- Ruler measurements (inches, centimeters)

- Daily schedule components

- English words and their foreign language counterparts

- Parts of speech

- Clock face and hands

- Coins and matching values

Source: Sandy Vono, Teacher, Plymouth, CT

nimal Toss

Auditory review and drill are common to most classrooms. Animal Toss is an active alternative to these auditory tasks. In Animal Toss small stuffed animals are passed from student to student as they take turns answering questions. Students who are tactile or kinesthetic learners especially benefit from this hands-on, physical activity. Animal Toss also increases motivation for all students, as it seems more like a game than work.

Recommended Grades: 1 - 6

How To

1. Obtain one or more small, soft, stuffed animals. (Beanie Babies are ideal for Animal Toss.)

2. Ask students to clear their desks or table tops.

3. When beginning a period of review questions or drill (e.g., math facts, spelling, vocabulary, or state capitols), explain that you will ask a question and then toss the animal to a student. (Students are more likely to listen and think if you pose the question before tossing the animal.)

4. Once the student has answered the question (with or without help from peers), he or she stands up.

5. Pose another question. This time the standing student tosses the animal to any other student.

6. Repeat the Animal Toss until all questions have been answered, or until all students have had a turn.

More Ideas

> &ampx; If small stuffed animals aren't readily available, try a foam rubber ball or other lightweight, soft object.

≈ If room permits, have students stand and form a circle prior to the Animal Toss. Students who purposefully throw wildly can sit out for the remainder of the game.

Source: Kathryn Barnwell and Regina Hall, Emerson Elementary, Cartersville, GA

Clear Desks

Many students see getting their first desk as a sign of entry into the world of "big kids." While desks do help students become more organized and attentive, desks can also increase problems for kinesthetic and tactile learners. Whether fiddling with what's inside the desk or constantly moving in the seat, learners who need movement often experience a decrease in organization and attentiveness when seated at a desk. Clear Desks, a strategy that empties desks of all material, provides kinesthetic learners the opportunity for purposeful movement throughout the day as they retrieve their materials from alternate locations. Clear Desks also helps tactile learners be more attentive by reducing the number of materials they may inappropriately fiddle with throughout the lesson.

Recommended Grades: 1 - 6

How To

1. Obtain boxes, milk crates, or other containers large enough to hold all the items from inside a student's desk.

2. Explain to students that many people work best with a Clear Desk. Describe adults in the school (or in literature) who fit this description. It is important that this be described as a learning style, rather than a problem that deserves punishment.

3. Select students who benefit from this strategy, especially tactile and kinesthetic learners.

4. Have students place all their belongings in their crates. Crates should be far enough away to provide students with an opportunity for movement, but close enough that they are not tempted to wander around the room on the way.

5. Give permission to students to put away and retrieve materials from their crates between activities. Direct students to only retrieve the materials needed and explain that as soon as the activity is over students may return materials to their crates.

More Ideas

- ❧ Younger or forgetful students may need specific directions about which materials to retrieve from their crates.

- ❧ For tactile learners, consider the Clear Desk strategy with Finger Feelers (see tactile strategy).

all Charts

Wall Charts are a wonderful alternative to requiring students to write at their desks. The Wall Chart strategy provides kinesthetic learners with movement to and from the charts and greater arm movement used in writing. All learners have the opportunity to stretch and get their circulation going. Wall Charts can be used by students for brainstorming, designing concept webs, figuring math problems, and many other activities typically done at their desks on paper.

Recommended Grades: 2 - 6

How To

1. Make sure there is clear access to four wall spaces in the classroom. Spaces should be far enough apart to allow ¼ of the students to congregate without being too close to other groups.

2. Post blank chart paper in the four wall spaces.

3. Hang wide-tipped markers on string beside each Wall Chart.

4. When ready to start, write a different question on each Wall Chart. Some examples are:

    ๛ "What is an example of a food from the grains food group?"

    ๛ "What is an example of a food from the dairy food group?"

    ๛ "What is an example of a food from the fruits and vegetables group?"

5. Divide students into four equal groups and assign each group to a Wall Chart to answer the questions.

More Ideas

๛ Combine Wall Charts with Graphic Summaries (Visual-Tactile Strategy) as an effective review strategy.

$\mathcal{G}$iant Steps

The greatest fear most teachers have when supplying students with kinesthetic opportunities is that students will end up running all over the room. Giant Steps are simple visual prompts that help to curb extraneous movement so that out-of-seat activities can be assigned. Giant Steps (large, laminated footprints) are placed on the floor to show students where to stand. While providing kinesthetic learners clear limits for movement, they also provide visual learners with visual input during standing activities.

Recommended Grades: Pre-K - 3

How To

1. Draw giant footprints (each approximately 18-by-24 inches) on bright paper. Laminate each footprint for longer life.

2. Adhere footprints to the floor wherever there is an activity which requires students to stand while they work. For example, if four students will be standing while working at a sand table, place footprints on the floor next to the table. Other activities might include working at chalkboards, overhead projectors, Wall Charts (see Visual/Tactile Strategy), or Standing Work Stations (see Kinesthetic Strategy).

3. Explain to students that they must stay within the Giant Steps if they wish to remain standing.

4. If several students will be allowed to work at an area simultaneously, place several pairs of Giant Steps there.

5. Explain to students that only one student may stand on a pair of Giant Steps. If the Steps are already filled, others cannot stand

there at that time. For example, during center time, students may be free to choose any one of five different centers (drama, sand table, overhead projector, reading corner, or listening center). Several pairs of Giant Steps are placed on the floor at each center. When these Steps are filled, students must choose another center.

Source: Steve Harland, OR

Stick-to-Me Apron

"All eyes on me" is a common phrase used by teachers to gain student attention. Wearing a Stick-to-Me Apron, or storyboard apron, is a wonderful way to reinforce and encourage student attention. Made from fabric to which Velcro will stick, a Stick-to-Me Apron is a walking, changeable storyboard. Symbols and pictures can be stuck to the Apron to draw student attention. Especially beneficial for visual learners, the Stick-to-Me Apron is novel enough to enhance learning for all students. Kinesthetic students often enjoy wearing Stick-to-Me Aprons, as it gives them the opportunity to stand and move around the room. Smaller Aprons can be made for students to wear.

Recommended Grades: Pre-K - 3

How To

1. Purchase a Stick-to-Me Apron (see Resources) or make one using an apron pattern and fabric to which Velcro will hook easily.

2. Purchase self-stick Velcro dots and hook Velcro at a craft or office supply store. Cut hook Velcro into one-inch squares.

3. Adhere the hook Velcro dots or squares to the back of such objects as:

    ❧ The RED/GREEN Circle — This cardboard circle (approximately three inches in diameter) is colored RED on one side and GREEN on the other. Stick the circle to the center of the apron with the RED side showing to indicate "Stop and look at me," or show the GREEN side to indicate "Get working." (The RED/GREEN Circle will need hook Velcro in the center on both sides.)

    ❧ The Letter of the Week — This is a large cardboard letter (for example, F) which students can see and discuss. The teacher may stick pictures or words on the Apron that begin with the same letter (e.g., fish, food).

- Noun/Verb Cards—Make a set of Noun/Verb cards using index cards. On a larger index card, write "VERBS." Stick the "VERBS" card to the Apron. On smaller index cards write verbs and nouns (one on each card). Adhere hook Velcro to the back of each. Ask students to choose verb index cards. When they choose correctly, stick them to the Apron.

- Math Cards—Create large cardboard numbers, "+", "-", and "=" cards. Cut out pictures that represent story characters or events. As you tell or read a story, stick and remove pictures from the Apron.

More Ideas

Give kinesthetic learners the opportunity to wear the Apron as "teacher's helper." Helpers can walk to students' desks and have their classmates stick items to their Apron.

esources

Books for Teachers

The Tough Kid Book by Ginger Rhode, William R. Jenson, and H. Kenton Reavis

> Research-validated solutions to reduce disruptive behavior without big investments in teacher time, money, or emotions. Also includes behavioral, academic, and social survival skills for students. Available from Sopris West (800) 547-6747.

The Tough Kid Tool Box: A Collection of Powerful Classroom Tools
by William R. Jenson, Ginger Rhode, and H. Kenton Reavis

> Provides elementary and middle school teachers with classroom-tested, ready-to-use materials for managing and motivating tough-to-teach students. Includes: Behavior Observation Forms, Mystery Motivator Charts, Self-Monitoring Charts, Contracts, and much more. Available from Sopris West (800) 547-6747.

Books for Students About Learning Differences

Alexander, H. (191). *Look inside your brain*. NY, NY: Grosset & Dunlap.

Barrett, S. (1992). *It's all in your head*. Minneapolis, MN: Free Spirit.

Levine, M. (1993) *All kinds of minds*. Cambridge, MA: Educator's Publishing Service.

Levine, M. (1990) *Keeping ahead in school*. Cambridge, MA: Educator's Publishing Service.

Perrin, J. & Santora, S. (1982). *Elephant style*. St. John's University, Center for the Study of Learning and Teaching Styles, Jamaica, NY 11439.

Smith, S. (1994). *Different is not bad, different is the world*. Longmont, CO: Sopris, West.

Children's Books About Learning Styles

Elephant Style by Perrin & Santora (1982). Jamaica, NY: St. John's University. (Fiction)

The bookfinder: A guide to children's literature about the needs and problems of youth aged 2 and up by S. Dreyer (1994). Circle Pines, MN: American Guidance. (A comprehensive reference material.)

All kinds of minds by M. Levine (1993). Cambridge, MA: Educator's Publishing Service. (Fiction)

Different is not bad, different is the world by S. Smith (1994). Longmont, CO: Sopris West.

Seven blind mice by E. Young (1992). NY: Scholastic. (Fiction)

About learning by B. McCarthy (1996). Barrington, IL: Excel. (Poems and quotes for discussion.)

Look inside your brain by H. Alexander (1990). San Diego, CA: Turning Point.

It's all in your head by S. Barrett (1992). San Diego, CA: Turning Point.

Books Including Poetry about Learning Styles

McCarthy, B. (1996). *About learning*. Barrington, IL: Excel.

Learning Style Instruments

For additional information on the Learning Style Inventory, contact:

> Center for the Study of Learning and Teaching Styles
> St. John's University
> Utopia Parkway
> Jamaica, NY 11439

For additional information on The Reading Style Inventory, contact:

> National Reading Styles Institute
> P.O. Box 737
> Sysosset, NY 11791-0737
> (800) 331-3117

For additional information about The Learning Type Measure, contact:

> Excel, Inc.
> 23385 Old Barrington Rd.
> Barrington, IL 60010
> (800) 822-4628

Additional Resources

For more information on the Carbo Recorded-Book Method, refer to *How to Record Books* by Marie Carbo. National Reading Styles Institute (800) 331–3117.

Tapes with classical musical selections are available from The Brain Store (800) 325-4769. Ask for "Better Thinking with Mozart" or "Baroque Music for Learning and Relaxation."

Highlighting Tape is available from Crystal Springs Publishing (800) 321-0401.

Hot Covers are available from Staples Office Supply (800) 333-3330.

To purchase a Stick-to-Me Apron, contact Book Props at (800) 636-5314.

Therapy Balls are available from Kennedy Professional Supply, (800) 272-4471.

For additional information on the use of Therapy Balls see: Spaulding, A., Kelly, L. Posner-Mayer, J. & Santopietro, J. (1998) *Kids on the ball*. Champaign, IL: Human Kinetics.

Seven minute tapes are available for use with Walkman Wonders from National Reading Styles Institute at (800) 331-3117.

References

Andrews, R.H. (1990) The development of a learning styles program in a low socioeconomic, underachieving North Carolina elementary school. *Journal of Reading, Writing and Learning Disabilities International*, 6(3), 307-313.

Armstrong, T. (1994) *Multiple intelligences in the classroom*. Alexandria, VA: ASCD

Armstrong, T. (1987) *In their own way*. New York: Putnam's.

Armstrong, T. (1995) *The myth of the ADD child*. New York: Dutton

Barber, L., Carbo, M. & Thomasson, R. (1994) *A comparative study of the reading styles program to extant programs of teaching reading*. Syosset, New York: National Reading Styles Institute.

Bauer, E. (1991) *The relationships between and among learning styles perceptual preferences, instructional strategies, mathematics achievement, and attitude toward mathematics of learning disabled and emotionally handicapped students in a suburban junior high school*. Doctoral dissertation, St. John's University, NY.

Brunner, C. & Majewski, W. (1990) Mildly handicapped students can succeed with learning styles. *Educational Leadership*, 48(2), 21- 23.

Butt, Tina (1997) Lecture titled "Connections of the mind: Integrating intelligence, brain and style research with multiple intelligences into effective teaching models," presented at the annual conference of the Association for Supervision and Curriculum Development, Baltimore, April 23, 1997.

Caine, R.N. & Caine, G. (1997) *Education on the edge of possibility*. Alexandria, VA: Association for Supervision and Curriculum Development.

Callan, R.J. (1998) Giving students the right time of day. Educational Leadership, December/January, pp. 84- 87.

Carbo, M. (1979/1994) *Reading Style Inventory*. Syosset, NY: National Reading Styles Institute.

Carbo, M. (1989) *How to record books*. Syosset, NY: National Reading Styles Institute.

Dunn, R. (1988) Commentary: Teaching students through their perceptual strengths or preferences. *Journal of Reading* 31, 4: 304-309.

Dunn, R. & Dunn, K. (1993) *Teaching secondary students through their individual learning styles: Practical approaches for grades 7 - 12*. Boston: Allyn & Bacon.

Dunn, R., Dunn, K., & Perrin, J. (1994) *Teaching young children through their individual learning styles: Practical approaches for Grades K-2*. Needham Heights, MA: Allyn & Bacon.

Dunn, R., Dunn, K., & Price, G.E. (1977) Diagnosing learning styles: Avoiding malpractice suits against school systems. *Phi Delta Kappan*, 58(5), 418-420.

Dunn, R., Dunn, K. & Price, G. (1989/1994) *Learning style inventory*. Lawrence, KS: Price Systems.

Dunn, Giannitti, Murray, Geisert, Rossi & Quinn,. (1990) Grouping students for instruction: Effects of individual vs. group learning style on achievement and attitudes. *Journal of School Psychology, 130* (4), 485-494.

Gardner, H. (1993) *Multiple intelligences: The theory in practice*. New York: Basic Books.

Gardner, H. (1997) Remarks made at the 69th Annual International Conference for the Association for Supervision and Curriculum Development, Baltimore, MD.

Goodlad, J.I. (1984) *A place called school: Prospects for the future*. New York: McGraw Hill.

Gregorc, A. (1982) *Gregorc Style Delineator*. Columbia, CT: Gregorc Associates.

Hodgin, J. & Wooliscroft, C. (1997) Eric learns to read: Learning styles at work. *Educational Leadership*, 54(6), 43-45.

Huggins, P. (1993) *Teaching friendship skills*. Longmont, CO: Sopris West.

Jensen, E. (1997) *Brain compatible strategies*. DelMar, CA: Turning Point Publishing.

McCarthy, B. (1981*) The 4MAT System: Teaching to Learning Styles with Right/Left Mode Techniques*. Barrington, IL: Excel.

McCarthy, B. (1993) *The Learning Type Measure*. Barrington, IL: Excel.

McCarthy, B. (1996) *About Learning*. Barrington, IL: Excel.

Myers, I & Briggs, C. (1975). *Myers-Briggs Type Indicator*. Consulting Psychologists Press: Palo Alto, CA.

Mohrmann, S. (1990) *Reading styles progress report*. Syosset, N.Y.: National Reading Styles Institute.

Price, G. (1980) Which learning style elements are stable and which tend to change over time? *Learning Styles Network Newsletter, 1*(3) 1.

Restak, R. (1979) *The brain: The last frontier*. New York: Doubleday.

Silver, H., Strong, R. & Perini, M. (1997) Integrating learning styles and multiple intelligences. *Educational Leadership*, 55(1) 22 - 27.

Snyder, A. (1994) On the road to reading recovery. *The School Administrator* 51, 1:23-24.

Spaulding, A., Kelly, L. Posner-Mayer, J. & Santopietro, J. (1998) *Kids on the ball*. Champaign, IL: Human Kinetics.

Yong, F. & McIntyre, J. (1992) A comparative study of the learning style preferences of students with learning disabilities and students who are gifted. *Journal of Learning Disabilities*, 25(2), 124-132.